Two and Two Make Sex

A Comedy

Richard Harris and Leslie Darbon

A SAMUEL FRENCH ACTING EDITION

SAMUEL FRENCH
FOUNDED 1830

SAMUELFRENCH.COM
SAMUELFRENCH-LONDON.CO.UK

FOR PRODUCTION ENQUIRIES

UNITED STATES AND CANADA
Info@SamuelFrench.com
1-866-598-8449

UNITED KINGDOM AND EUROPE
Theatre@SamuelFrench-London.co.uk
020-7255-4302

Each title is subject to availability from Samuel French, depending upon country of performance. Please be aware that *TWO AND TWO MAKE SEX* may not be licensed by Samuel French in your territory. Professional and amateur producers should contact the nearest Samuel French office or licensing partner to verify availability.

TWO AND TWO MAKE SEX

First produced by Ray Cooney, Productions Ltd.
at the Cambridge Theatre, London
on 30th August 1973
with the following cast of characters—

George	Patrick Cargill
Clare	Jane Downs
Nick	Richard Beckinsale
Jane	Barbara Flynn
Ruth	Diana King
Mr Bowers	Terence Alexander

The Play directed by Jan Butlin
Setting by Hutchinson Scott

The action takes place in the drawing-room of George and Clare Williams' house in Highgate, and Jane Bowers' bedsitter in Holland Park

ACT I   Scene 1   Wednesday evening, late summer
          Scene 2   The following morning
          Scene 3   The following Wednesday evening

ACT II   Scene 1   Wednesday evening, two weeks later
          Scene 2   The following Saturday morning

Time—the present

TWO AND TWO MAKE SEX

ACT I

SCENE 1

The drawing-room of George and Clare Williams' house in Highgate, and Jane Bowers' bright and sunny bedsitter in Holland Park. Wednesday evening, late summer

The drawing-room, which occupies the larger area, is an elegant room, with an alcove at the rear. This alcove is on a small raised area which has steps leading down into the main room. Outside the alcove is a suggestion of a hallway. There are large french windows leading out onto the garden, with the suggestion of a terrace outside; a telephone on a table, a drinks cabinet, a sofa, occasional tables and chairs, a drinks table

The bedsitter is on a raised platform, with a door in the rear wall and, outside, the suggestion of a hall with stairs leading down. On the door is a coat hook. An alcove leads from one wall to the unseen kitchen and bathroom. There are a double bed, a cabinet with a reading lamp, and a mirror above, shelves jam-packed with books, a small record-player, a large inflatable white plastic chair and, on the floor next to it, a telephone. Above the bed is a large poster advertising a Spanish bullfight. The room is very untidy, scattered with books and crockery

As the CURTAIN *rises, only the bedsitter is illuminated*

Nick sits on the bed, quickly taking off a huge pair of silver-painted Tuf Boots. He stands, pulls back the bedcovers, thrusts the boots deep into the bed and pulls the covers over them. He is quickly tidying the bed when Jane enters, wearing a topcoat. She reacts on seeing him, clearly not expecting him to be there

Jane You're not supposed to *be* here.
Nick (*holding up a placating hand*) I'm just going.
Jane If *you* think you can spoil my evening . . .
Nick Never entered my mind.
Jane (*sarcastically*) Ho-ho.

Jane looks at him for a moment then exits through the alcove

As soon as she has gone, Nick reaches under the bed and pulls out a long blue-and-white football supporter's scarf and a rattle. He hangs the scarf on the door-hook, winding it round several times to make removal difficult, looks at the rattle, not sure where to put it—and rams it amongst the books on a shelf

Jane returns, now minus the topcoat

Nick puts on a pair of tatty tennis shoes

And don't come back before ten o'clock.

Nick I could stay out all *night* for all the good it'll do you.

Jane (*putting her face close to him*) Try me.

Nick What would he tell his wife?

Jane How do you know there *is* a wife?

Nick There's *always* a wife. He'll be on the phone to her this very minute— making an excuse about where he'll be tonight—*betcha*.

Jane You haven't got anything to bet *with*.

Nick Lend us a bob.

Jane (*almost exploding*) Why do I put up with you?

Nick (*with a flat smile*) Because you need me.

Jane *Need* you?

Nick And because you need me you resent me.

Jane Despise. (*She vaguely begins to tidy the room*)

Nick And so what do you do? You find someone to taunt me with— someone who, in your eyes, is my exact opposite.

Jane *Right*. A very sensitive human being.

Nick (*generously*) It's just a phase you're going through. I *understand*. And because I understand it won't work.

Jane What won't work?

Nick You trying to make me jealous. (*He grins*)

Jane looks at him scornfully and exits through the alcove with a plate piled with orange peel and a quart bottle of beer

(*Calling after her*) Me—jealous—ha! (*He quickly reaches up, swings the bullfight poster round to reveal a sign which reads "Trespassers Will Be Violated"*)

Jane enters

Nick moves quickly from the poster

Jane Then why don't you go to your pathetic evening class?

Nick I'm collecting my books. (*He collects up a pile of paperbacks to prove his point*)

Jane You're trying to ruin my evening with George.

Nick (*seizing on it almost maniacally*) Ah! *George*, is it? (*He struts around, doing what he fondly believes to be an imitation of a "George"*) Good Old George—I can see him now—coming through that door—bowler hat—bunch of flowers—bottle of plonk—crippled with arthritis and riddled with guilt. It's perfectly obvious to me that he's—he's . . .

Jane The word you're searching for is "mature".

Nick If he's so mature—why haven't you told him about *me*?

Jane Because he's a very sensitive human being.

Nick There's no need to make excuses.

Jane (*angrily*) Will you please *go*!

Nick (*oh-so-calm*) On my way. (*He almost goes but turns*) And another thing—lend me ten P for the bus?

Jane picks up her handbag to hurl at him

Nick scarpers through the door, closing it behind him

Jane fumes for a moment, then glances at her watch and quickly resumes tidying the room. She collects up a tray of used crockery and exits to the kitchen. There is a loud crash and she enters, sees the scarf on the door, moves to unravel it

Jane Pathetic. You really *are* pathetic.

Jane crosses to the cupboard unit to open a door and push in the scarf. A mountain of junk tumbles out. It includes a set of chest expanders, an artist's palette and oil brushes. She is ramming it all back in when the doorbell rings. She freezes momentarily, then checks herself in the mirror, moves to the door, sees the poster, jumps up on the bed to swing it round to reveal the bullfight advertisement. The doorbell rings again as she jumps down from the bed, hurries to the door, composes herself, then opens the door calmly

George is standing in the doorway. He wears a bowler hat, three-piece suit. Both hands are behind his back

Their initial conversation is bright but desperately strained

George Not too early, am I?

Jane (*looking briefly at her watch*) Twenty-five to seven. Perfect.

George Only we did *say* half past six.

Jane That's what I mean—twenty-five to seven. Perfect.

George I suddenly had awful visions of you—you know—dashing home from the office—tidying up . . .

Jane Oh, no. I'm a very tidy person. By nature. Won't you—er . . .? (*She indicates "come in"*)

George Thank you. (*He comes in*)

Jane closes the door

For *you*.

He pulls a small bunch of flowers from behind his back. She takes them, reaches up, kisses his cheek

For *us*.

With the other hand he produces a bottle of red wine. He bends to kiss her, remembers, removes his hat; then kisses her cheek

Jane (*of the flowers*) I'll—put these in water.

Jane exits through the alcove

George looks around: clearly it's the first time he has been here. He puts his hat on the bed and then, rather furtively, presses the bed to test its springiness

Jane puts her head round the door

Do make yourself comfortable.
George Thank you.

Again little smiles

Jane exits

George perambulates somewhat, putting the wine down on the cupboard unit. And then catches sight of himself in the mirror. He quickly checks his appearance, paying particular attention to what he fears might be a receding hairline. He starts pulling a bit of hair forward with his fingers

Jane enters with the flowers in a pot

Immediately his hand moves from his head and sweeps along a row of the books

I notice you read.
Jane (*a shade too fast*) Oh yes—avidly. (*She is clearly edgy about the books*)
George They say you can tell a great deal about people by the books they read.
Jane (*putting down the flowers*) Yes.
George Let's see what I can find out about *you*. (*He taps various books*) *Astronomy For Beginners*.
Jane I've always been keen on the stars . . .
George *Sheepdog Training*.
Jane I've always been keen on animals.
George The *Kama Sutra*.
Jane I've always been keen on . . . I think I must have borrowed that one.

They "laugh". George continues to run his finger along the row of books— stops—pulls out the blue and white football supporter's rattle—looks at her and gives the rattle a couple of slow twirls

(*A little "laugh"*) I don't always read. Sometimes I watch football.
George Do you really?
Jane Yes: I love it.
George Which team do you support?
Jane Queens Park Rovers.

George Rangers.
Jane Yes. (*She remembers*) Glasses.

Jane exits quickly to the alcove

George replaces the rattle and takes out a slim paperback next to it.

George (*calling*) I say—this looks interesting—*The Psychology of Human Relationships.*
Jane (*off*) Oh—yes—fascinating.
George (*flipping at the book*) D'you think I might borrow it?
Jane (*putting head round the alcove*) Sorry?
George (*holding up book*) This.
Jane (*misconstruing*) Oh—yes. *Please* sit down.
George Thank you.

Jane's head disappears. George moves across, slipping the book into a pocket. He almost sits on the bed, but changes his mind and moves to the low plastic chair—looks at it dubiously, raises it off the ground. Clearly it is the first time he has met one

(*About to sit, calling*) I must say you've made it very comfortable here. (*He sits in the chair and immediately nearly topples over backwards. He rolls about, regaining his balance*)

Jane enters carrying two glasses and a bottle opener

George immediately gets up ("rolls out" is probably a better way of putting it) and takes the opener from her. He takes up the bottle but somehow doesn't quite get round to opening it

("*Off-hand*") You're quite sure it's—all right—you know—my coming here?
Jane How long have we known each other?
George Two months.
Jane (*taking his arm*) Two months. And this is the first time you've been here. That's what makes it all right. *More* than all right.

She kisses him briefly. He moves to sit at the foot of the bed, pats the bed for her to sit next to him. She does so. He looks at her terribly sincerely, still using the bottle opener vaguely

George You know, what's so—marvellous—about our relationship is that we know so little about each other—and yet so much.
Jane That's what makes it—us—different. *I* know just enough about *you*— and *you* know just enough about *me.* Any more and it wouldn't be . . .

She searches for the right word, looks into his eyes for help, so that they are staring at each other

George (*helpfully*) Us?
Jane Yes—that's it—that's exactly *it. Us.*

George Us.
Jane Yes.
George (*continuing his help*) *Other* people . . .
Jane But we're *not* other people . . .
George We're *us.*
Jane We're *you.*
George And *me.*
Jane No questions.
George No demands.

A moment

God, it's marvellous.

He finally pops the cork from the bottle. Jane fetches the two glasses and returns to sit at his feet on the floor. He pours wine into the glasses, puts the bottle on the floor. They toast each other

Jane Here's to British Rail. You missing your train.
George And here's to British Weather. You forgetting your umbrella.

They sip their wine. She cradles her head into his lap. He somewhat tentatively reaches down to stroke her hair

Jane George . . .
George Yes, Jane?
Jane George . . .?
George Yes, Jane?

Suddenly she sits upright, knocks back her wine and is clambering up to kiss him passionately, forcing him back on the bed. His right arm jerks upright as he tries not to spill his, wine. He lets out a yell. She releases him suddenly and sits upright

Jane (*with her head turned away*) I shouldn't have done that.
George No, I understand . . .

He reaches deep into the bed and pulls out Nick's boots. They both stare at them for a moment

Jane I told you: I watch football.
George (*very sincerely*) I understand.

She takes the boots delicately from him and pushes them under the bed

Jane That's what I *mean* about you—you're so—understanding. So—mature.

He knocks back his wine and takes her hand

George The last thing I want you to think is that our—affair—is just a—physical thing.
Jane That's exactly how *I* feel.
George It hasn't been easy . . .

Jane I know . . .
George There *have* been times . . .
Jane I know there have . . .
George But there's more to life than just—the body.
Jane Much more.
George Jane?
Jane Yes, George?

For a brief moment they are looking at each other. And then, in a sudden explosion of activity, George is on his feet pulling off his coat—Jane is moving round to pull back the bedcovers, in doing so, knocking George's hat to the floor. George pours her a glass of wine—can't find his own glass so swigs directly from the bottle—so that they are drinking—undressing—helping each other to undress—with much more effort than actual result. The effect should be of comic confusion rather than sexiness. So that George is minus coat, waistcoat, tie—Jane minus blouse and skirt. He is about to take off his trousers but sees that she is sitting on the bed taking off her shoes, so he does the same.

George (*about to pull off a sock*) I haven't phoned my wife.
Jane Phone?
George To say I'd be late home.
Jane George, she's your wife.
George I'll do it straight away.
Jane Yes, that's a very good idea. George—I can't—I mean I wouldn't . . .
George I'll phone her now.
Jane I just couldn't, not if I thought she'd be worried about you . . .
George How could I have been so thoughtless.
Jane You do understand don't you?

He hobbles across to the telephone, kneels, and dials as Jane exits through the alcove to reappear a moment later pulling on a housecoat. George finishes dialling. We hear a telephone ringing out

The immediate area around the telephone in the drawing-room is spotlighted: the rest of the room remaining in total darkness

George cups the receiver, turns, looks at Jane. They blow little kisses at each other

Clare enters to take up the telephone in the drawing-room

Clare Hello.

Immediately George uncups the receiver. Jane sits on the bed

George Is that *you*, Clare?
Clare Yes of course it's me, George.
George The thing is, I don't want you to worry. (*He turns and gives a confident little nod to Jane*)
Clare I'm not worrying, George: why should I worry?

George Yes of course you are. The thing is—look, I'm awfully sorry—I'm
   going to be late.
Clare I know you are.
George *Yes.*
Clare You phoned to tell me half an hour ago.
George Yes. The thing *is*—I'm with this client. The car broke down—and
   British *Rail*—well I mean, it's absolutely absurd.
Clare George.
George Yes, Clare?
Clare I'm *not* worried. I *know* you're going to be late. I'll expect you when
   I see you. 'Bye. (*She replaces the receiver. Stands for a moment, hand on
   receiver. Then, she sighs*)

The drawing-room light fades

*Meanwhile, George shoots a quick glance at Jane who is studiously looking
elsewhere and then—as though still having a telephone conversation.*

George ("*concerned*") Oh. I see. I'd completely forgotten. Yes of course
   I will. No. Yes. As soon as possible. Good-bye, Clare. (*He hangs up*)

Jane, hearing the change of tone in his voice, stands up

   I'm afraid I've made a terrible mistake.
Jane What kind of mistake.
George I don't know how to tell you.
Jane Try.
George There are people coming to dinner. An important client and his
   wife. In half an hour.
Jane You must go.
George Yes.

*For a moment they stand looking at each other. Then they start to dress—
at almost the same rate as they undressed*

   I feel so *guilty.*
Jane Of course you do—she's your *wife.*
George I mean about leaving *you*—*here*—*alone.* Would you mind passing
   me that shoe?
Jane This one?
George Thank you.
Jane There'll be other times.
George Me going home to a wife and you having no-one.
Jane I've always known the situation. (*She turns her back on him*) Zip.

*He quickly looks down at his zip-fly, but realizes she means the zip of her
blouse. He zips her up*

   You've never lied to me, have you?
George Never.
Jane And *I've* never lied to *you*, have I?
George Not once.

Jane Then that's all that matters.

She pulls a long hair from his coat. He stares at it

George But I *worry* about you.

They both attempt to inspect his clothing minutely

Jane Then you mustn't.

George I'll try.

Jane If you worry, it will *show*. And if it shows, your wife will find out. And if she does, there'll be no more—*us*. Because I couldn't—and neither could *you*, could you?

George No. Is my tie straight?

She adjusts his tie and then sniffs his shoulder. He immediately slaps a hand to the shoulder

What is it?

Jane Oh. (*She sniffs*) Scent.

George (*worried*) Anything? (*He sniffs*)

Jane Not a trace. You must go.

She leads him to the door

And promise me you won't worry.

George Promise.

Jane For *her* sake.

They kiss briefly

George Lunch on Friday—same place?

Jane Super.

She opens the door. He almost goes, but turns

George You *do* understand—about tonight.

Jane I respect you for it.

Again he almost goes

And George.

George Yes?

Jane Remember—it would ruin everything if she ever found out.

George Don't worry, she'll never know.

A flurry of blown kisses and George exits

Jane closes the door on him, leans against it, and slowly puffs air from her cheeks

The lights dim in the bedsitter and simultaneously the drawing-room lights come up

Clare is at the drinks cabinet, fixing two drinks. Ruth sits, lighting a cigarette.

Clare carries the drinks over, hands one to Ruth. They sip the drinks. A moment. Ruth is clearly waiting for Clare to say something

Clare George is having an affair.
Ruth *George?*
Clare Why the surprise? You of all people. You must get a thousand letters a week saying more or less the same thing. "Dear Aunt Ruth. My husband is having an affair and what the hell do I do about it?"
Ruth Not exactly thousands. And certainly not about George.
Clare He's a very attractive man.
Ruth Very.
Clare To a great many women George would be—well—quite a catch.
Ruth A catch indeed.
Clare Then why shouldn't he?
Ruth What?
Clare Have an affair.
Ruth Who are you trying to convince—you or me?
Clare I *am* convinced. (*Slight pause*) I think . . . Yes, of course I am.

A moment

Ruth Are you confiding in me as a friend—or consulting me as a specialist?
Clare As a friend.
Ruth Ah.
Clare But only because you're a specialist.
Ruth All right. You think George is having an affair.
Clare Yes.
Ruth I'll need a little more to go on than that.
Clare (*as though reading aloud*) All right, I'll write you a letter. "Dear Aunt Ruth. *My* husband is a changed man."
Ruth In what way?
Clare "In many ways. First, there's his vest."
Ruth What *about* his vest?
Clare He's stopped wearing one. Apart from the first six months of our marriage, he's *always* worn a vest. Winceyette, with buttons.
Ruth *George?*
Clare He has what he calls a British Chest. It rumbles.
Ruth How fascinating.
Clare Not when you're lying in bed next to it it isn't. Secondly, there's his running.
Ruth His running.
Clare Round the park. "Six months ago he got breathless just *looking* at the lawnmower and now he goes running round the park. In a yellow tracksuit and black and white training shoes." Frankly he looks like a cross between George Raft and a decrepit canary. "Then there's the sauna bath."
Ruth He goes to a sauna bath.
Clare No, he wants to *install* one. *Here.* In the garden. (*She points*) "Then there are the gramophone records."

Ruth He's always been rather fond of Oscar Hammerstein.

Clare Not any more. Look here, Clare, he said: "Why don't you pop out and get something with it? Something by that lady, Alice Cooper."

Ruth And *did* you?

Clare I went the whole hog. (*She shows Ruth a record*) Four young men called The Spew.

Ruth I assume they were out on parole.

Clare Quite.

Ruth Does he play it?

Clare I caught him *once*. There was a look of blank amazement on his face.

Ruth I'm not surprised.

Clare As soon as he saw me he started to hum—and give him credit, it's not easy humming to someone shaking a corrugated iron sheet. (*She knocks back her drink, sighs, takes Ruth's glass and replenishes both*) "My husband is clearly trying to impress someone and since he gave up trying to impress *me* years ago, it therefore follows he has someone else in mind. And more than likely in *body*." (*She hands Ruth her glass*) Cheers. (*She drinks*)

A moment

Ruth "Dear Reader. You omitted to mention one very important detail. How *old* is your husband?"

Clare Forty-nine next birthday—but don't you dare tell him I said so.

Ruth Precisely. George is purely and simply undergoing what is known in the trade as The Virility Crisis. Or putting it another way—he's afraid of growing old.

Clare He *can't* be growing old. *I'm* not.

Ruth He's a man, he's forty-eight, and he's suddenly aware of it. I bet he even combs his *hair* differently.

Clare No—but he *has* grown the most amazing side-whiskers.

Ruth Well there we are. The time-honoured middle-aged man's little game. "Redistribution of Visible Assets." I'll even bet he's thinking of changing his car.

Clare It's being delivered next week.

Ruth A sporty little broom-broom, no doubt.

Clare An MGB. (*With an awful thought*) An MGB and no vest. He'll *freeze* to death.

Ruth Well—there's my answer, Clare. George has reached the virility crisis. It happens to *all* of them. I know. It happened to my husband.

Clare (*knowing full well*) And what did *he* do about it?

Ruth (*sighing*) Found himself a little dolly and ran off with her.

Clare And *you're* telling *me* not to worry.

Ruth I'm telling you that George is exhibiting well-worn symptoms but it doesn't necessarily follow that he'll do any more than run round the park and build himself a sauna bath.

Clare Then how about *these* symptoms? For the past two months he's been coming home late every Wednesday with the most ridiculous

excuses about where he's been. And it's not as if I *ask* him. He comes
bursting through that door, brandishing a huge bunch of flowers,
chuntering nineteen to the dozen. Every Wednesday the same thing.
Today was absolutely typical. He starts off by mumbling something
about a problem over breakfast . . . phones at ten to say he *might* be
late—phones again at three to say he *will* be late—by six o'clock he's
got a world *crisis* on his hands. If *that's* not another woman, I don't
know what *is*. (*After a slight pause, touched*) Poor George. He will *try*
so hard. (*Rather sheepishly*) I even marked his socks.
Ruth Marked his *socks*?
Clare So that I'd know if he'd taken them off. (*With a weak smile*) Evidence.

Ruth shakes her head, smiling ruefully. Clare sighs

Ruth Clare, you want my professional advice—ask him. Bring it out into
the open.
Clare I couldn't.
Ruth (*with a shrug*) That's what I'd tell my readers.
Clare But I'm *not* one of your readers.
Ruth Thank you.
Clare You know what I mean. I'm not words on a page, I'm someone
you've known for years. (*A moment*) He's not the only one who's finding
out he's not young any more.

Pause

Ruth Right. So. You're not absolutely *sure* there's someone else, are you?

For a moment Clare seems about to argue

Clare (*eventually*) No.
Ruth Then let's assume he's putting out warning signals. That he's saying—
look, pay more attention to me or something *might* happen.
Clare I *do* pay attention to him.
Ruth Perhaps not the right sort.
Clare We've been married twenty *years* . . .
Ruth Exactly. Marriage is like a bath. The longer you lie in it, the colder
it gets.
Clare And so it needs—(*She mimes turning a tap*)—topping up?
Ruth Better *your* hand on the tap.
Clare Perhaps *I* need topping up too.
Ruth (*smiling*) Perhaps you just need a bigger bath. (*Indicating her glass*)
May I?
Clare Please do. You may be right. Warning signals. Yes, I'll improve
myself. (*She nods absently*)

Ruth fixes herself a drink

Ruth (*smiling to herself*) He'll look rather dashing in a sports car. (*She
drinks*)
Clare And his yellow tracksuit.

Ruth With his whiskers blowing in the wind.
Clare He's a very attractive man.

Slight pause

Ruth How *is* your personal life?
Clare You mean . . .?
Ruth Yes.
Clare Well—it's not exactly the raging fire it *was*—but there's still the odd glow amongst the embers.
Ruth So fan the flames a little.
Clare Fan the flames and run the bath.

We hear the sound of a car arriving and stopping

(*Worried*) You've just called in.
Ruth (*laughing*) Don't worry—I know exactly what he thinks about *me*.
Clare For a chat.
Ruth What?
Clare A chat. You just called in for a chat.
George (*off, calling*) Darling, I'm home!

George enters, carrying a huge bunch of flowers

Clare (*brightly*) Ah, there you are, darling. Ruth's here. She just dropped in for a chat.
George (*harrassed*) What?
Clare (*pointing with her glass*) Ruth.
George Oh.
Ruth Hello George. (*She smiles sweetly*)

Clare carries the drink across to Ruth. As she does, George stands looking at them suspiciously. But he assumes a big smile as Clare returns

Clare Drink?

George smiles at her, but as she mixes his drink, he whispers

George What's *she* doing here?
Clare (*brightly*) She was just passing and thought she'd drop in.
Ruth For a chat.
George (*to Clare*) What *sort* of chat?
Clare Oh—you know—just a chatty sort of chat.

She hands him his glass. He realizes that he still holds the flowers

George For you.

She takes them, kisses him, behind his back indicating the flowers to Ruth as if to say, "you see?"

Clare Darling—you shouldn't have. (*She sniffs them and puts them down*
George A little coming home present.
Ruth A little Coming Home *Late* Present.

George ("*laughing*") Yes. (*With a hiss*) What is she *doing* here?

Clare flicks something from his coat shoulder. Immediately his hand goes to it

What's wrong?

He moves quickly to examine himself in the mirror. Ruth and Clare exchange a quick glance

Clare I thought I noticed a little tear.

George Tear? There? Never. It's a snare. In the material. I'll phone that damned tailor first thing in the morning.

Clare It's probably just a loose cotton.

George That's no excuse. There's too much of this shoddy workmanship about nowadays. (*He drinks quickly*) That's why I'm late. You get in a car and it doesn't *work*—you get in a train and it doesn't *go*—and the food—my god—they call that *food*?

Ruth *Do* they?

He glares at her, then knocks back his drink, pours himself another one

George Did you get my phone call?

Clare Now let me think . . . (*She feigns trying to remember*) Yes—yes—I think I *did*.

George Good!

Clare As a matter of fact, I got all *six* of them.

George Yes—well—you know—I like to keep you informed—things being as they are—rushing about—up down up down—I thought—you know —ring Clare—keep in touch—don't want her to worry.

Ruth How very considerate.

Clare It's amazing you found time to have the car repaired.

George Car.

Clare Message Number Six. "With this client—car broke down . . ."

George Not *my* car—*his* car.

Clare Oh, you went in *his* car.

George Yes of course. Didn't I say?

Clare It was the one thing you forgot to mention.

George How silly of me.

Ruth How *is* the property business?

George (*stiffly*) Fine. And how's the Agony Column?

Ruth Flourishing, I'm sorry to say.

George Sorry? I thought you were at your happiest meddling in other people's affairs.

Ruth ("*smiling*") Sweet.

George Who are we today—Sister Goodheart or Auntie Ruth?

Ruth Neither actually. (*Smiling*) Madame Zenda.

Clare The Stars and *You*.

George ("*impressed*") Oh, that's *you* as well, is it? I read you only yesterday as a matter of fact—and you were absolutely right. I *did* get a letter. From my *son*.

Ruth Where *is* he now?
George Don't you know? Rub a bit of Windowlene on your crystal ball.
(*He lights a cigarette*)
Ruth You've never forgiven me, have you?
Clare Don't start him on *that* one.
George What's there to forgive? I'm delighted. What father *wouldn't* be?
Ruth He simply asked my advice. He wanted to see the world.
George And *you* said: "Why not? It will broaden your mind." And how
is he *doing* it? Sitting cross-legged, halfway up a mountain in the
Himalayas, staring at some Indian vicar's *feet*.
Ruth (*calmly*) Make your point, George.
George My point, Sister Bigmouth, *is* that if my son wanted to study
chiropody, why couldn't he do it at an English University like everyone
else does?
Ruth Do they?
Clare George has this thing about higher education.
George Not as high as the Himalayas. George has this *thing* about other
people meddling in his family affairs. (*Sweetly*) Are you staying for din-
ner?
Ruth Unfortunately I have a prior engagement.
George Too bad.
Clare That reminds me—dinner. Excuse me.

Clare exits

George Don't hurry your drink. (*He thrusts Ruth's glass into her hand*)
Ruth George—have you ever wondered why you're so rude to me?
George It's something I never question.
Ruth Perhaps you should read Freud.
George Perhaps I will. Just as soon as I've (*He mimes*) waved you and your
revolting cigarettes good-bye.

*Ruth finishes her drinks, stands, collecting up her handbag. She looks at him
for a moment*

Ruth (*in a very different tone of voice*) George. I *understand*.

*She momentarily squeezes his arm. He looks down at her hand and then back
up again with total incomprehension*

Clare enters at almost the same moment

I must go. (*She moves to the door*)
Clare (*moving with Ruth*) I'll give you a ring.
Ruth Do.

Ruth and Clare exit

George (*disparagingly*) Freud. (*With a change of tone*) Freud. (*He takes the
paperback book from his pocket and sits down, opens the book at random.
After a moment*) Fascinating. Absolutely fascinating.

Clare enters

Clare What is?
George This book.

As Clare moves in we see that she is holding a pair of carpet slippers

The Psychology of Human Relationships.
Clare What made you buy that?
George Buy it? Err—I just happened to be browsing through this book-shop--in Cambridge—you remember I told you I've been to Cambridge today—and I thought—that looks very interesting. So I bought it.

As he speaks he slips the book behind the cushion at his back, while Clare gets on her knees and pulls off his shoes

What are you *doing*?
Clare Putting on your slippers.
George *I* can do it.
Clare No, no, no . . .

He stares down as she puts on his slippers but it is obvious she is far more interested in his socks

It's the least I can do. Hard day in the office—*and* in Cambridge—car, train, food . . .
George (*amazed*) What are you doing with my *socks*?
Clare I was just thinking how well they fitted you.
George Almost like a glove.
Clare Mitten. Let me get you another drink.

She goes and fixes him another drink. He stares down at his slippered feet

George Incidentally—guess who phoned today?
Clare You.
George Yes. No—phone *me*—in the office. (*He beams*) Old Jack.
Clare (*flatly*) Good Old Jack.
George He's coming down in a couple of weeks. I invited him for lunch. Saturday the fourteenth.
Clare Couldn't you have said we're busy?
George Not Old *Jack*. We haven't seen him for *ages*. (*She gives him the drink*) Anyway, I thought you liked him.
Clare He makes passes at me.
George That's what I thought you *liked*.
Clare What I *don't* like is the sight of the pair of you, half-drunk, tears in your eyes, singing those awful rugby club songs. (*She mimes holding a pint and, in macho-bass, sings one of the awful songs she's talking about*)

George takes up the song happily, but stops and:

George (*sighing*)They don't write songs like that any more.
Clare Oh, I don't know.
George Anyway—he's coming on the fourteenth. Put it in your diary.

A moment

Clare George?
George Yes?
Clare I was wondering. How would you feel about a bigger *bath*?
George What!?

He looks at her in blank amazement

The lights dim in the drawing-room and simultaneously come up in the bedsitter

Jane sits at the head of the bed, knees up. She hears someone whistling in the hallway and immediately slides down into a languorous lying position, one hand behind her head, gazing dreamily up at the ceiling

Nick enters. He carries a pile of books and is whistling somewhat inanely. He pulls a key from the lock, stuffs it into a pocket, moves across to dump the books carelessly on the cupboard unit. He glances briefly at Jane who studiously dreams up at the ceiling. He sees the pot containing George's flowers, takes it up

Nick Huh!

He puts down the pot, and whistles his way out through the alcove. Only now does Jane turn her head in his direction, but looks sharply back at the ceiling as he enters, swigging from a bottle of milk

I've had a great idea. Can't fail. Rodney Marsh Hairgrips. I can see it now. Every footballer in the country wearing a Rodney Marsh Hairgrip. Blue—with *his* signature. In gold. (*He leans close to her*) You've got to admit, it's a winner.
Jane Like all your ideas.
Nick The only reason for my failure to date is general apathy on the part of The Great British Public.
Jane Talking of general apathy—what have you *done* today?
Nick You know perfectly well. I've been to my evening classes.
Jane And what are we on *this* week?
Nick Ah! Your apparent lack of memory is due, purely and simply, to a sub-conscious rejection of my thirst for learning.
Jane You think so.
Nick Definitely.

Throughout the following, she takes up the books he brought in, and one by one tosses them at him after glancing at the title. He gathers them and defends himself at the same time

Jane Since I've known you, your thirst for learning has taken in—*Food Reform for Health Nuts—Car Maintenance for Owner-Drivers—Japanese Flower Arrangement—The Use and Care of the Automatic Sewing Machine*—and now—which brings us back to the sub-conscious rejection bit—*Advanced Psychology. Not,* you notice, Psychology. *Advanced* Psychology yet.

Nick (*smug*) What you are exhibiting now is a typical pattern of aggression.
That is, a manifestation of The Will To Power—as according to Adler—
or a projection of The Death Impulse—as according to Freud.
Jane (*with face close to his*) Nick?
Nick Yes?
Jane *Knickers.*

Jane exits through the alcove

Nick grimaces after her, then quickly starts to search the bed for his boots

Jane appears in the alcove, holding the boots at arm's length

Looking for *these*?
Nick *Me?* What? Huh!
Jane Pathetic. You really *are* pathetic.

Jane drops the boots disdainfully and exits

Nick moves quickly to take up the boots and examine them

Jane returns

Nick quickly puts the boots down

Nick Have a nice time then?
Jane (*sarcastically*) I thought you'd never ask.
Nick I knew how disappointed you'd be if I didn't.
Jane Thank you: I had a *wonderful* time.
Nick Good.
Jane I take it we're eating out?
Nick You mean *George* didn't feed you?
Jane We had better things to do.
Nick Very *good.*
Jane I'm glad you approve.
Nick Anything in particular.
Jane Amongst *other* things, we had a deep and meaningful discussion.
Nick God, he sounds like Harold Wilson. In fact I bet he *looks* like Harold
Wilson.
Jane I'm hungry. Where're we going? (*She opens the door, starts to exit*)
Nick (*going after her*) I thought we'd go to this little Greek place I found.
Bags of atmosphere. Wonderful food. You'll like it . . .

Nick reaches the door, scowls into the room, then follows Jane off

The lights come up in the drawing-room.
Clare, in a sexy housecoat, is at the open french windows
Clare (*turning in to the door*) It's all right—you can go now—it's dark.

George enters. He wears his yellow tracksuit and his training shoes

George (*"jogging"*) Whatever you may think, Clare—I am not ashamed of being seen.

Clare Off you go then.

George I am simply—limbering—*up*. (*He jogs towards the french windows*)

Clare George—do stay away from Wakefield Crescent.

George That ridiculous woman—calling the police.

Clare She was *frightened*, George.

George And that policeman—I *ask* you—a breathalyser test.

Clare Wouldn't it have been awful if your tracksuit had turned green?

George (*glaring but with dignity*) Please run my bath.

George jogs out through the windows

Clare waves him good-bye, and stands at the windows. After about ten seconds, we hear the sound of two dogs barking angrily, and George shouting at them

Clare (*shaking her head sadly*) Oh dear. (*She moves to sit in the chair George sat in earlier. Uncomfortable, she reaches behind the cushion and brings out the book. She looks at it*) Psychology. (*She shakes her head slightly and flips at the book. Suddenly her attention is drawn to the inside cover*) Holland Park Bookshop? He said *Cambridge* . . . (*She quickly flicks through the book and opens it at the back cover*) Stolen from Nicholas Craig. Seven two seven, oh seven four five . . .? (*She frowns, sits for a moment, then closes the book. She sits looking ahead*)

Jane and Nick enter the bedsitter. She is furious. He is slightly drunk

Jane Little Greek place. A fish and chip shop run by a Cypriot.

Nick The gherkins were good.

Jane Bags of *atmosphere*.

Nick Well—at seventy-five the two, you can't complain.

Jane *I* paid, *I* can complain. Isn't it about time you got a *job*? (*He undresses, throwing clothes around untidily*)

Nick I wrote for one only last week.

Jane Managing Director of I.C.I.

Nick That's what is known as Positive Thinking.

Jane Apparently *they* didn't think so.

Nick I can't understand it. My references were marvellous.

Jane A letter from your mother does not constitute a reference.

Nick She said some very nice things about me.

Jane (*very angry now*) I really don't know what I see in you.

Nick Come off it—you're fascinated by me—you always have been.

Jane I must have been mad, falling for a line like that. (*Brightly*) "Let's start a commune" he says.

Nick It was a very good idea.

Jane You didn't say it was going to be just you and *me*—in *my* flat.

Nick It's a start. (*By now he is down to red underpants and Mickey Mouse vest*)

Jane You're totally irresponsible.

Nick Not *totally*.

Jane And you *really* wonder what I see in George?

In the drawing-room, Clare looks at the book, gets up, moves to the telephone

Nick Have you ever thought that inside every boring old George there's an exciting young Nick just waiting to get out?

Jane And have *you* ever thought that inside every boring young Nick there's another Nick—even *more* boring?

Nick What you are exhibiting now is a typical case of Transference?

Clare, after hesitating, starts to dial slowly, referring to the back cover of the book

Jane Nick, if you give me any more of that psychoanalytical crap, I'll . . . I'll—(*taking up pot of flowers*)—I'll transfer these clothes right out of the window.

Nick exits through the alcove, smiling sweetly

Nick (*as he goes*) I *understand* . . . I *understand* . . .

Jane glares impotently down at the pot. The telephone rings. She snatches it up

Jane Doctor Nickel-arse Craig's Psychiatric Clinic. Nutcase Number One speaking.

Clare (*into the receiver*) I beg your pardon?

Jane Doctor Nickel-arse Craig. Psychiatrist—psychoanalyst—psychopath. You name it, he'll analyse it.

Clare So sorry. I must have the wrong number. (*She hangs up, stands for a moment, then moves back to sit, staring down at the book*)

At the same time, Nick enters with a towel

Nick Who was that?

Jane Wrong *number*.

Jane snatches the towel from him, shoves the pot into his hands, and exits through the alcove

Nick puts down the pot, looks from it to the telephone

Nick Bloody *George*.

At this moment, George staggers in through the French windows. He is exhausted

Nick gets into bed in vest and pants

Clare (*brightly*) Had a nice run?

George is too breathless to reply, try though he might. He crosses to pour himself a drink. As he does, we see a great rip in the seat of his tracksuit

Nick turns the poster round to reveal the "Trespassers Will Be Violated" side

George sees that Clare has his book

George (*breathlessly guiltily*) What are you doing with my book?

Clare Just—you know—having a little read (*Brightly*) Did you know that whistling was a sign of virility?

George (*guilt uppermost*) That's *my* book—my book . . .

Clare (*nervously*) Yes, all right, George—don't worry—I'll—run your bath.

Clare exits, still looking at George rather nervously

George slumps exhausted into a chair, wincing when his backside makes contact

Nick in bed, leans across for his cigarettes, sees something on the floor, reaches down to take up George's hat. He looks at it, looks inside

Nick (*reading*) George Williams. George *Williams. Right,* Mister Williams. (*He gives the hat a Karate-chop and rams it on his head, sits with arms crossed*)

Jane, in nightgown, enters. She reacts on seeing the hat, but chooses to ignore it. She gets into bed

At the same time, Clare enters the drawing-room, still looking at George doubtfully

George sits, chest heaving. Clare sits. For a moment there is silence: Jane and Nick sitting up in bed—Clare and George sitting in chairs. Then, at the same time but to varying effect, George and Nick begin to whistle

SLOW CURTAIN

SCENE 2

The same. The next morning.

The lights come up in the bedsitter.

An alarm clock is ringing—muffled, but loud enough to wake a sleeping person. Jane, in bed with Nick, stirs and raises her head from the pillow. With an effort she manages to stagger out of bed in search of the alarm clock. She looks in the cupboard, behind the books, shifts the flower pot, etc., before turning to Nick and shaking him.

Jane Where have you put it?

Nick does not move a muscle. Jane gets on her knees and pokes under the bed, searching. After a moment, she pulls out the suitcase and takes out one of those enormous alarm clocks that are about ten inches in diameter. She switches it off and leans over Nick

Wake-Wakey. The Great British Public is waiting to be bowled over by your brilliance.

She crosses to the curtained off corner wardrobe and takes out the clothes she needs for the day. She sees clearly that Nick has no intention of shifting himself

Incidentally, Mr Psycho-analyst. Did you know that the inability to rise early is a sign of a waning sexual urge?

Jane exits to the kitchen

A moment

Nick shoots out of bed like a rocket and follows Jane

The lights cross fade to the drawing-room

Clare sits, in housecoat, pouring coffee. George enters, minus jacket, clearly aching in every limb. He sits painfully

George I shall sue. That's what I shall do. Sue.
Clare You can't sue a dog.
George It's *owner*.
Clare You must have done something to upset it.
George Creatures like that shouldn't be roaming the streets at night.
Clare That's what that lady in Wakefield Crescent said about *you*.
George Stupid woman. (*A thought*) It was *her* dog. A savage reprisal.
Clare You're so *emotional* lately, George.
George I am not emotional, I am scarred. Permanently scarred.
Clare It adds character.
George You're absolutely right. It's the one thing I've always wanted: a characterful backside.
Clare I'm the only one who'll ever see it. (*A moment*) Aren't I?
George That is not the . . . (*Changing his tone*) Yes of course you are, darling. Absolutely right. I'm being ridiculous. Absolutely ridiculous. I don't think I want any coffee. (*He stands*) I think I'll get off to the office. (*He gets into his jacket which was lying across a chair*)
Clare (*helping him*) I can't find your hat anywhere.
George My hat—it must be . . . (*Suddenly*) My *hat*. (*He pulls away, stares at her*)
Clare Yes, George—your *hat*.
George I don't want you to worry—*please*—don't worry.
Clare Perhaps you left it somewhere.

George I haven't *been* anywhere—*nowhere.*
Clare You've been to Cambridge.
George Cambridge?' (*Quickly*) Yes. I left it in the car.
Clare I've already looked in the car.
George Why? I mean why should you look in the car? What made you do *that*?
Clare (*worried by his "neurosis"*) Because every morning, I give you your hat. It's a sort of ritual. You *like* your hat. It's your full-stop.
George Full-stop? (*Suddenly*) Did you look in the boot?
Clare The *boot*?
George Please. Look in the boot.
Clare (*worried, but pacifying*) Yes of course I will, darling. Now stop worrying.
George *I'm* not worrying. It's just that I don't want *you* to worry.
Clare (*as though to a child*) All right George—I'll—look in the boot.
George Don't worry, Clare, don't worry. I don't understand, I had my head, I must have had my hat.

Clare exits, distinctly worried

As soon as Clare has gone, George goes to the telephone and dials quickly. The bell rings in the bedsitter

The bedsitter lights up

Jane is making up before the mirror. She crosses to answer the telephone

Jane Hello?
George (*with a hiss*) I must see you.
Jane Who *is* this?
George (*with a hiss*) *George.*
Jane (*looking towards alcove*) See me?
George Stay where you are—I'll be straight round.

George slams down the receiver. Jane looks at the telephone, worried, then lowers it

After a moment Jane exits through the alcove

Clare enters the drawing-room

George still has his hand on the receiver. He snatches it up again

Yes, I'm still here. You have? Good. I'll be straight round. (*He rams down the receiver*)
Clare It isn't there.
George No of course it isn't. I just phoned the Lost Property Office. At the station. *They've* got it. I must go there immediately.
Clare But it's only a *hat*, George.
George It may only be a hat to *you*, but to me, it's a lost hat. And lost hats are hard to find.

George exits haughtily. Clare exits after him

Jane and Nick enter through the alcove. He is wearing George's hat, with a flower sticking from it

Nick *Sausages?*
Jane (*taking up her purse*) Pork.
Nick *Now?*
Jane I'm doing—Toad in the Hole.
Nick (*delighted*) My favourite.
Jane Yes—I want to get it prepared before I leave for the office.
Nick Specially for *me*?
Jane Yes.

Jane gives him money, takes the hat from his head, hangs it on a doorhook, and exits to the alcove. Nick exits, taking down the hat en route and ramming it on his head. He closes the door

Clare and Ruth—carrying a briefcase—enter the drawing room

Ruth Your husband nearly ran me down.
Clare (*her mind elsewhere*) He couldn't find his hat.
Ruth Came out of that drive like a madman. *Hat?*
Clare It seems to be on his mind.
Ruth (*with an edge*) Not on his *head*.
Clare Yes. (*Suddenly*) Why are you here?
Ruth (*slightly taken aback*) What? I was on my way to the office, I—just thought I'd pop in—after our little chat last night—see if—well, if anything had *happened*.

Clare looks at her for a moment, then moves to pick up George's book

Clare (*about to refer to the book, then changing her mind*) I think I might have misread the whole thing.
Ruth Misread? (*She looks at the book*)
Clare George's—(*waving the book*)—goings-on.
Ruth (*carefully*) In what way?
Clare I don't know. (*She looks at the book*) Perhaps two and two *don't* make four. Perhaps they make six.
Ruth What are you *talking* about?
Clare Well—perhaps it *does* add up—George's—goings on—but not in the way we *thought* it did.
Ruth (*not with it*) I'm sorry—it's rather early in the morning and I haven't had any coffee . . . (*She pours herself a cup of coffee*)
Clare —I think he might be ill.
Ruth (*nodding*) It's all that running.
Clare (*shaking her head*) In the head.
Ruth You mean . . .?
Clare (*nodding*) I think he might be having treatment.
Ruth *George?*

Clare If he *was*—you know—*ill*—it would account for a lot of things, wouldn't it?

Ruth But he would have *told* you.

Clare Not necessarily. And yet perhaps in a way, he *has:* perhaps that's why he keeps telling me not to worry. (*She sits, looks at the book*)

Ruth Look—if there's anything I can *do* . . .

Clare Should I get in touch with him?

Ruth Who?

Clare The psychiatrist.

Ruth You *know* who he is?

Clare I—happened to find out. (*Uncertainly*) Perhaps it was deliberate. A *clue*. A cry for help. These things often happen, don't they? (*She guides Ruth to the door*)

Ruth (*positively*) If *you* think George is having treatment and can't tell you, then it's perfectly reasonable for you to have a—well, a quiet word— with his—psychiatrist.

Clare and Ruth exit

The doorbell rings in the bedsitter. Jane answers it

George enters breathlessly

Jane What's wrong?

George My hat—I left my hat.

Jane (*relieved*) Oh—your *hat* . . .

She reaches up behind the door. The hat has gone. George moves nervously into the room

George It's little things like that she notices. She was a journalist, you know.

Jane (*with a sudden bright thought*) The thing is—I sent it to the cleaners.

George The *cleaners*?

Jane It'll be ready tomorrow . . .

George But I must have it today—I'm at the Lost Property Office collecting it—she *knows* I am.

Jane Tell her—tell her it got dirty. I mean—stuffed in with all those suitcases.

George (*starting to argue, then changing his mind*) You're right. There are some filthy travellers in this world—*she* knows that. (*Convinced*) It's at the cleaners. (*He kisses her cheek*) I must go.

Jane So must I.

George I'll give you a lift. (*He opens the door*)

Jane Thanks.

Jane exits. George makes to go after her, but sees the "Trespassers" notice, stares at it briefly, and then exits, still puzzling over it

Ruth and Clare enter the drawing-room

Ruth (*collecting her briefcase*) Darling, I must fly—but you *will* let me know . . . ?
Clare Of course I will.
Ruth Thanks for the coffee—and don't *worry*.

Ruth exits

Nick enters the bedsitter, still in the hat, brandishing a package

Nick (*calling*) Sausages! (*No answer*) Jane? (*He looks into the alcove*) Well I like *that*. (*He shrugs, tosses the package onto the bed and moves to sort through his book collection*) I'll do it m'self . . . (*He takes a book from the shelves and moves away, flicking through it*) Toad In The Hole . . .

In the drawing-room, Clare moves to the telephone and dials

(*Reading the book*) Toad In The Hole. "First catch toad. Place toad in hole . . ." (*He hurls the book away*)

The bedsitter telephone rings. Nick lifts the receiver

Hello?
Clare (*tentatively*) Is that Doctor Nicholas Craig?
Nick (*grinning, but deep-voiced*) The same.
Clare I'm terribly sorry to trouble you, doctor: it's about my husband.
Nick Is it?
Clare I'm—Mrs George Williams.
Nick George . . . ? (*He takes off the hat, looks inside it, stuffs it back on his head*) Oh yes, Mrs Williams?
Clare I understand you're treating him?
Nick Did *he* say that?
Clare No. It was in your book.
Nick Book?
Clare I mean I think he left it as a sort of *clue*.
Nick Which particular book would it—
Clare (*referring to the book*) *The Psychology of Human*—
Nick —*Relationships*. (*With a satisfied smirk*) So *that's* where it went.
Clare That's how I found your number. The thing is, doctor—I know it's unethical—but he *is* my husband—and I'm worried about him.
Nick I bet you are.
Clare Tell me: is it serious?
Nick Serious enough.
Clare Poor George. (*Firmly*) I want to help.
Nick (*playing the full "doctor" now*) Now you mustn't worry, Mrs Williams. He'll pull through. But there's no doubt that he needs careful handling. Which is why I'm glad you phoned.
Clare Perhaps I should come and see you.
Nick Good—*good* . . .

Clare When would be convenient?

Nick Just let me consult my diary . . . (*He puts down the receiver, gleefully rubs his hands together, and moves away*) Nurse—let me see my diary, will you? (*In a "nurse's voice"*) Yes, Doctor Craig. (*In a "doctor's voice"*) Tell the other lunatics to wait, will you, nurse.? (*He tosses the package of sausages in the air and catches them in George's hat. Then returns to take up the receiver*) Are you there, Mrs Williams?

Clare Yes, doctor?

Nick How about Wednesday? It will have to be evening . . .

Clare Wednesday evening—yes. He always goes out on a—but doesn't he come to see *you* on Wednesday evening?

Nick Ah! The thing is—this particular Wednesday—I've arranged for him to meet a colleague of mine. A specialist.

Clare (*worried*) In what?

Nick I thought you'd ask that. (*He gropes across the floor for a book and reads from it*) The Double Aspect Theory of Identity Hypothesis— Are you there?

Clare Yes.

Nick tosses the book away

Nick Not uncommon at *his* age.

Clare Would that account for his vest?

Nick takes the receiver from his ear, stares at it for a moment

Nick No doubt about it at all. *At all*. I'll have to come and see *you* then.

Clare If that's . . .

Nick Oh yes—absolutely. And the address again is . . .?

Clare Twenty-three Linchester Square, Highgate.

Nick (*jotting it down*) Twenty-three Linchester Square, Highgate. Seven o'clock.

Clare Fine.

Nick And—er—best not say anything to your husband, Mrs Williams. The last thing we want is for him to *worry*.

Clare (*nodding*) Seven o'clock then, doctor.

Nick Thank you for calling, Mrs Williams.

Clare Thank *you*, doctor.

They both lower their receivers simultaneously. A moment, then Nick takes up the hat, admiring it

Nick (*gleefully*) Gotcha! (*He thumps the crown of the hat*)

During this, Clare paces, concerned. Then in the same moment, they move to their telephones and dial. They wait a moment

Clare Mr Williams, please.

Nick Miss Bowers, please.

A moment

Clare George?
Nick Jane?
Clare ⎫ It's *me.*   ⎰ *speaking*
Nick ⎭   ⎱ *together*

A moment

Clare Sorry to bother you, darling—
Nick I was wondering—
Clare ⎫ —*about next Wednesday*—   ⎰ *speaking*
Nick ⎭   ⎱ *together*

A moment

Clare ⎫ Will you be out?   ⎰ *speaking*
Nick ⎭   ⎱ *together*

A moment. Then they both smile

SLOW CURTAIN

SCENE 3

The same. The following Wednesday evening

Only the bedsitter is illuminated

George sits, drink in hand, trying to get comfortable in the plastic chair. He gets up and idly moves round the room—sees the wall poster which now depicts the Bullfight—stares at it—is about to discreetly look at its other side when Jane enters through the alcove, wearing a small apron. They "smile" at each other

Jane Won't be long.
George Fine—fine.

Jane exits

George "rolls" out of the chair

Jane enters

Jane You're sure you don't mind eating in here?
George (*on his knees*) Not at all . . . not at all . . .

Jane smiles and exits

George gets up and goes to look through the alcove

George It looks very . . . romantic.

Jane appears, they kiss briefly and she exits

George perambulates a little

(*Remembering*) Oh yes—I've brought your book back.
Jane (*off*) Oh. Yes.
George (*taking the book from pocket*) I must say it's absolutely fascinating. Fascinating.
Jane (*off*) Yes.
George Err—*yes*.

A moment. Then he clears his throat and starts to whistle a clearly-rehearsed "When My Sugar Walks Down The Street". He crosses to the bookshelves, looks at the book, puts it on a shelf and in the same moment stops whistling

Jane enters, takes up a bottle of wine, moves to the alcove and turns

Jane Did you know that whistling is a sign of virility?
George Oh really?

Jane exits

*George, confidence boosted, attempts "The Flight of the Bumble Bee".
It is a mistake*
(*Calling, "off-hand"*) I—er—I think I'll just give her a ring.

Jane (*off*) Yes—we don't want her to worry.

George moves to the telephone and starts to dial

The drawing-room lights come up

Nick, in suit and glasses, is thumbing through the Penguin Dictionary of Psychology. He's clearly mugging up like mad. He has a drink to hand

Clare enters carrying a tray on which is a plate of sandwiches

Nick immediately rams the book into a pocket, stands, and takes the tray from her

Clare I assumed you were coming straight from your clinic, so I made a few sandwiches.
Nick How kind—just a—*teeny* bit peckish—*you* know . . .

Nick puts a whole sandwich in his mouth and eats hungrily as the telephone rings

Clare (*moving to the telephone*) Excuse me.

As soon as her back is turned, Nick starts wolfing the sandwiches

Hello?
George Is that *you*, Clare?
Clare Oh, hello, George . . .

Nick almost chokes on his sandwiches, but waves a hand indicating for her to play it cool. He continues to wolf, but listens attentively

George The thing is—I'm with this client. For some incredible reason, he wants to *eat.*
Clare (*looking at Nick*) You're with a client and he wants to eat.

Nick nods, holds up a wise finger

George The thing *is*—he's just *come*—from Nairobi.
Clare Nairobi.
George Apparently the food on the plane was appalling.
Clare On the plane.
George You don't mind then?
Clare No, no—you go ahead and enjoy yourself.
George Yes. (*Correcting himself*) Hardly *enjoy*. Just—*eat. Eat.*
Clare *Eat.*
Nick Thank you.
George Food—and—*things*. I'll probably give you a ring later.
Clare No, no, George—don't worry.
George Yes. 'Bye, Clare.
Clare 'Bye, George.

They both hang up

Jane appears in the alcove

Jane All right?
George No trouble.
Jane She didn't . . .?
George Not a thing.
Jane (*smiling*) Then let's eat.

Jane holds out a hand. George crosses, takes her hand, and they exit through the alcove

The lights dim in the bedsitter

Nick Nothing wrong is there, Mrs Williams?
Clare No, no—it's just that I was expecting someone a little—
Nick —older?
Clare (*tentatively*) Frankly—yes.
Nick As a matter of fact—so was *I*. (*He gives a little laugh*)
Clare (*flattered*) Oh. Do sit down and I'll get you a drink.
Nick Thank you.

As Clare pours a drink, Nick hurriedly gets a chair and positions it carefully to one end of the sofa

Clare I know he doesn't want to tell me he's with a colleague of yours but those lies are so obvious.

Nick Would you mind lying, Mrs Williams?
Clare I beg your pardon.
Nick On the couch.
Clare Oh I see. Why?
Nick Why? Good question. The first thing is—they always lie on the couch.
It's the first thing they teach us: get your patient horizontal.
Clare But I'm not your patient.
Nick Ah! (*Guiding her to the sofa*) But you must be my patient so that
through you I can delve into the narrow recesses of your husband's
tiny mind.

He gets her to lie full-length

Now. I want you to close your eyes—empty your mind—and think
back way back as far as you can—way—way—way—back.

She does so

Now. Where are you?
Clare Sainsbury's.
Nick Good. Good.
Clare Forgive me asking, doctor—but is this really helping George?
Nick Don't worry Mrs Williams, I'll help George.
Clare What exactly is he suffering from?
Nick It's what's known in the trade—profession—as—(*delving into his
book*)—manic-depressive-psychosis. A mental disorder which alternates
between periods of excitement and periods of depression—sometimes
with intermediate periods of sanity.
Clare Yes, that sounds like George.
Nick Good.
Clare What causes it?
Nick His age and certain disturbing factors—for example . . .
Clare He was terribly upset when our son left home.
Nick Ah! Your *son*.
Clare *Yes*.
Nick Was he an only child?
Clare *Yes*.
Nick You have no daughter?
Clare No. He always wanted a daughter.

Nick gets up, puts the book in his pocket, moves round, looks down at her

Nick I think he's *found* one.

She sits upright

Clare Oh. (*Barely controlled*) What?

From now on, she barely conceals "The Woman Betrayed"

Nick Now I know it's come as a shock. But you must see that what this—
woman—represents to your husband—is a daughter-replacement-
figure.

Clare How *old* is this replacement-figure?
Nick I'm not sure. But I think she's twenty on the fifteenth of September.

Clare gets up and moves around

Clare Then there *is* another woman.
Nick Think of her not as a woman—but as a symbol.
Clare A symbol.
Nick Yes.
Clare A daughter-figure.
Nick Yes.
Clare Of twenty.
Nick Now. We must decide on a course of action.
Clare I already have.
Nick Yes?
Clare I'm going to kill him.
Nick Understandable. But it won't help *George*.
Clare It'll do *me* a lot of good. (*She sits next to him, picks up a sandwich and savages it*)
Nick I'll be very frank with you, Mrs Williams. I—as a psychiatrist—have done all I can to explain to him exactly what he's going through.
Clare What he's going through is nothing to what he's *going* to go through.
Nick The thing is, we must free him of this woman.
Clare Don't worry Doctor, I'll free him.
Nick Only then will he return to his usual state of sub-normality.
Clare (*fuming*) Daughter-figure.
Nick You know—you're very attractive when you're angry.
Clare Am I really?
Nick I was hoping when I came here tonight—bearing in mind the sort of woman I thought you'd be—to bring about an immediate solution to the problem. I now see—bearing in mind the sort of very attractive woman you are—that we'll need to spend a lot more time together.
Clare Well—if you really think so, doctor . . .
Nick Oh I do, I do—and—er—call me Nicholas—most of my patients do—it—er—it helps the relationship.
Clare (*smiling*) Nicholas.

For a moment they are smiling at each other. Then he stands and looks at his non-existent wristwatch

Nick Which reminds me—I wonder if I might telephone one of my patients?
Clare Of course.
Nick (*going to the telephone and dialling*) A rather neurotic little creature—likely to do something she'll regret at any moment.

The bedsitter lights come up

George is entering backwards from the alcove pursued by an amorous Jane. She forces him onto the bed. He is clearly fighting a losing battle. The telephone rings. Immediately she gets up to answer it. George sits up. He is clutching a stick of celery. He chews on it lifelessly

Jane Hello?
Nick (*still as "the doctor"*) It's me.

Throughout this, Clare pours herself a drink and paces upstage: the tigress

Jane (*shooting a look at George; brightly*) Oh—hello—*Sue*.
Nick I take it your friend is with you?
Jane (*still bright*) All the way, *Sue-dear*.
Nick Good—good—just checking.

Nick hangs up, glowers, unseen by Clare. Jane hangs up

Jane (*to George*) Just a chum. Coffee?

Jane moves towards George. He stands, arms outstretched, ready for an embrace

But Jane moves straight past and into the kitchen. George sighs and exits after her, taking another bite of celery

The bedsitter lights dim

Nick Thank you, Mrs Williams.
Clare Why don't you call me Clare?
Nick Thank you—Clare.

They smile at each other

You—er—you mentioned my book. Might I have it?
Clare And to think I thought it was a cry for help.
Nick Oh *no*. Kleptomania.
Clare You mean he *stole* it?
Nick A typical symptom. Quite normal.
Clare Oh.
Nick I must go.
Clare No don't go, Nicholas. (*She takes his arm*) Stay and have some coffee.
Nick (*looking at his arm, a little over-awed*) Well—(*He clears his throat*)—thank you.

She smiles and moves to the door

Clare Come into the kitchen while I make the coffee, we can carry on with our little chat.

Clare smiles and exits. A moment, and then Nick moves after her. En route, he takes up an ashtray and slips it into his pocket

Nick (*calling after her*) Yes. A kleptomaniac. Quite normal . . .

Nick exits

The bedsitter lights come on

Jane enters through the alcove. George somewhat wearily follows her. She looks at him. He tries on a rather weak smile

Jane It's no good.
George Isn't it?
Jane We're too close.
George But I thought . . .
Jane To *her*.

George opens his mouth to protest, then changes his mind

George I understand.
Jane I know you feel exactly the same.
George Very *true*.
Jane Somehow, the—the—*ambience* is all wrong.
George (*not really understanding*) Yes.
Jane If only we could . . . (*She trails off*)
George Could?
Jane (*shaking her head*) I mustn't.
George You mean . . .
Jane Don't say it.
George Get away together.
Jane You shouldn't have said that.
George I couldn't stop myself. (*He makes to grasp her hand but finds he is still clasping the celery*)
Jane (*turning to him*) Could we?
George What?
Jane Get away together?
George You shouldn't have said that.
Jane I couldn't stop myself.
George We've come—too far.
Jane *Don't.* (*She sits on the plastic chair*)

George sits next to her and takes her hand

George We fought against it.
Jane But we lost.
George There's no turning back. (*He kneels before her and in doing so, knocks a knee on the telephone causing much pain to himself which he tries to conceal*)
Jane We'd have to plan it very carefully.
George What?
Jane Our weekend together.
George Our weekend. Oh—*yes*.
Jane How will you do it?
George Err—I'm seeing a client.
Jane Where?
George Rotherham.
Jane Paris.
George *France?*

Jane We mustn't rush into it.
George I'll start sowing the seeds tonight.
Jane She mustn't—
George —not a thing.
Jane The last thing I want—
George —I know.

A moment

Jane It *had* to happen, George.
George I know—I know. Jane?
Jane Yes, George?

He gazes long and sincerely into her eyes

George (*in the same voice*) May I use your phone?
Jane I'll make some more coffee.
George Lovely.

Jane kisses his cheek and exits to the alcove

George rubs his knee, and dials the telephone

Nick enters the drawing-room, goes to the telephone, and dials at the same time that George does

They both wait, receiver to ear. We hear the engaged tone. They both frown slightly, lower receivers, stand a moment

George exits to the alcove

Clare enters the drawing room

The bedsitter lights fade

Clare (*referring to the telephone*) All right?
Nick No. My patient—*needs* me. I'll have to . . .
Clare Of course. But about George: all it boils down to is that he's a manic-depressive-psychotic with a tendency for stealing things.
Nick Yes.
Clare And *only* that.
Nick Yes.
Clare Oh good.
Nick The thing *is*, Mrs—er—*Clare*—I think we should meet again. Next Wednesday.
Clare But won't *he* be seeing you next Wednesday?
Nick Him? Oh—ah—*no*. He'll be having treatment with my colleague for the next two or three weeks—er—don't ring *me*, I'll ring *you*. (*He jots down the phone number on a slip of paper*) If on the other hand you *should* ring me—*have* to—which I hope you *won't*—you might find my

nurse rather strange. Now don't worry about this: you see, she's an
ex-patient. I—er—I'm keeping an eye on her. She's a rather sad case.
Clare I'll wait to hear from *you* then.
Nick Fine—*fine*—and of course we won't say anything to—er—George—
about this evening. George—or anyone, for that matter. (*He takes her
hand comfortingly*) And remember, you mustn't worry.

The doorbell rings. He starts

Who's that?
Clare I've no idea.
Nick Could it be . . .?
Clare No—we would have heard his car. Excuse me.

Clare exits

*Nick, worried, hurries to the drinks table, grabs a bottle of Scotch, cannot
find a glass so takes a huge swig from the bottle. It burns his throat so he
grabs the soda syphon and squirts some into his mouth. He shakes his head
violently from side to side, "mixing" his drink*

Clare and Ruth enter

They look at Nick. He gulps down his drink

Nick (*in his "doctor's voice"*) Good evening.
Clare Nicholas Craig—Ruth Sharples.

Nick moves to pump Ruth's hand

Nick Delighted to meet you. (*To Clare*) Must go, you will excuse me,
won't you?
Clare I'll see you out.
Nick No, no, I can manage. (*Going to door*) Good night.
Clare ⎫ Good night ⎰ *speaking*
Ruth ⎭   ⎱ *together*

He stands, smiling, not quite able to make an exit, but finally makes it

Clare and Ruth sit on the sofa

Ruth *Well.* What a very dishy young man.
Clare Very. You mustn't say he was here.
Ruth Not a word, darling: who *is* he?
Clare George's psychiatrist.
Ruth (*with an edge*) *I* see.

*Ruth lights a cigarette, looks for an ashtray. Clare makes to fetch her the
ashtray taken by Nick, reacts on finding it missing, fetches another one*

Clare There *is* another woman. No—not *woman*—*girl*—*twenty*.
Ruth Oh. (*A moment*) So we're back to two and two making four.

Clare We're back to two and two making *sex*.
Ruth What are you going to do?
Clare Kill him.
Ruth After you've killed him.
Clare After I've killed him. (*She almost fumes then calms herself*) Take *your* advice, I suppose: have it out with him.
Ruth But not in the mood you're in.
Clare I can't see it changing. A *woman*—yes. But a *girl*. It's a bloody insult.
Ruth (*sighing*) I agree.
Clare All right, what do I do?
Ruth Well the *last* thing you do is set yourself up as the villain of the piece.
Clare Meaning?
Ruth Meaning that if you stop him seeing this girl he'll probably resent it for the rest of his life.
Clare So what am I supposed to do—let him see *more* of her?
Ruth Yes.
Clare Thank you, Aunt Ruth. (*She throws up her arms in despair*)
Ruth Clare darling, he doesn't want to break up your marriage any more than you do. At the minute it's all marvellous for him—holding hands in the park—secret little dinners—what's more romantic than the stolen hour? *Hour.* But let him see *more* of her and things *might* not look quite so rosy. Believe me, romance takes a bit of a bashing over soggy cornflakes.

A moment

Clare And if it doesn't?
Ruth All right—it's a gamble—but if you want to tip the odds a little—you could always play him at his own game.
Clare I wouldn't know *how*.
Ruth (*smiling*) You'd learn, darling. Ask your psychiatrist friend.
Clare (*after a moment*) He *is* rather dishy.
Ruth Very dishy indeed.

They hear a car arriving

Ruth That sounds like George. I'd better go.
Clare Play him at his own game.
Ruth Love forty.
Clare Forty-*nine*.

George enters through the alcove, wearing his hat and brandishing a huge bunch of flowers. He moves straight to Ruth

George I'm terribly sorry, darling—first the plane was delayed ... (*He suddenly realizes who he is talking to, glares at her, turns and moves to Clare*) First the plane was delayed—then the customs—and the food at the airport—you have no *idea* ...
Clare (*very coolly*) Oh I think I *have*, George darling.

George (*referring to Ruth*) What's *she* doing here?
Ruth Just going. (*She moves past him*) Hello George.
George Still—interfering?
Ruth (*smiling*) I like to keep my nose to the ground.
George Unfortunately that leaves the other end of your anatomy in a
   rather vulnerable position.
Clare George is quite an authority on vulnerable ends.
George Yes. What?
Clare I've mended your tracksuit.
George (*almost angrily*) There's no . . . (*He breaks off*) Thank you, darling.
   (*To Ruth*) Good night, Ruth.

Ruth smiles and makes to exit

Ruth I'll look in again tomorrow, Clare . . .
George Don't bother.

   Ruth and Clare exit

George hurriedly checks himself in the mirror

   Clare enters

*George moves quickly away from the mirror, Clare picks up a book and
sits on the sofa. As he speaks, George goes and sits beside her*

   I really am most awfully sorry about tonight, darling. I mean—you
   know—airports—in out in out up down up down . . .
Clare (*very coolly*) George . . .
George Yes, darling?
Clare Knickers.

She "smiles" flatly at him. He stares at her

The lights in the drawing-room fade as the lights come up in the bedsitter

*Jane, in her housecoat, is pulling back the bedcovers, trying to make the bed
look slept in*

   The door opens and Nick comes in

*Immediately, Jane starts to make the bed, without looking at him. He moves
across and, behind her back, puts the ashtray on the cupboard unit. She
"notices" him, and double-takes*

Jane You're wearing a *suit.*
Nick Yes.
Jane I didn't know you had a *suit.*
Nick Yes.

   Nick exits into the alcove

Jane frowns a little, and lies on the bed

Nick returns with his milk and a mug. He pours the milk into the mug as Jane speaks

Jane (*"casually"*) There's some wine left.
Nick Is there?

He drinks his milk, starts to undress tidily—even uses a hanger for his jacket. She watches him with growing annoyance at both his tidiness and indifference

Jane Well?
Nick Well what?
Jane No psycho-analysis this evening?
Nick (*"surprised"*) No.
Jane Don't you want to know what we've been doing?
Nick No.
Jane (*trying to smirk it off, but unable to resist asking*) And where have *you* been?
Nick Didn't I say? Group Therapy Session.
Jane And did you learn anything—*fascinating*?
Nick As a matter of fact, I did.
Jane Which is . . .?
Nick Which is—that to a highly-sensitive young man—a highly-mature older woman—has a great deal to offer.

Nick exits jauntily through the alcove

Jane Just a *minute* . . .

Jane exits quickly after Nick

The lights in the bedsitter dim as the lights in the drawing-room come up

Clare sits knitting

After a moment George staggers in through the french windows. He wears his running kit, and is totally out of breath

Clare (*brightly*) Hello, George: had a nice run?

He tries to speak but cannot. He staggers across to pour himself a drink. We see that he has a large, conspicuous patch on the seat of his tracksuit

George, I think we should have a little talk.

He tries to answer, but can only nod

You've *changed*, George.
George (*just managing to speak*) Me?
Clare You're not the man I married.
George You can hardly expect me to be the same man after twenty years.

(*He bends behind the sofa and produces a set of chest expanders. He does various exercises throughout the following*)

Clare Quite. Let's face it, a lot of water has flown under the bridge since we first met.

George Flowed.

Clare (*smiling*) You see?

George How d'you mean—*changed*?

Clare I *understand*, George. Our marriage has become a habit. A nice habit—but a habit nevertheless. It's quite understandable for you to get bored.

George I'm not bored.

Clare Of course you are. And so am I. It's so—cosy. There's nothing left to fight for any more. And since Phillip left home, well—we've *done* it all.

George (*dumb-founded*) Well—I wouldn't go so far as to . . .

Clare Be honest, George. It doesn't mean to say we don't *love* each other—but—we need something extra now—a stimulus. That's why I think we should spend more time apart.

George lets the expanders collapse sharply

George Apart?

Clare It will do us good. Make us—appreciate—each other more.

George (*all he can think of*) But I *worry* about you.

Clare Then you *shouldn't. I* don't worry about *you.*

George Don't you?

Clare I *understand.* There are times when you want to be *free*—free to do what *you* want to do—like—like listening to records of The Spew—and I feel the *same*, George. And who knows *what* we might find?

George has the expanders behind his neck at arms' length. Suddenly they collapse, almost strangling him. He extricates himself with difficulty

George You go to *art* classes.

Clare It's not *enough.*

George (*trying a different tack*) As a matter of fact, there *have* been times when I've wanted to be . . .

Clare Free?

George Yes—*free.* I mean—for example—there's this client—now *he* wants me to go to Rotherham one weekend—this *coming* weekend—but I thought, no—you know—*Clare*—*weekend* . . .

Clare But you should *never* think like that, George. Especially if its business . . .

George Oh yes—it's *business.* Well it *would* be, wouldn't it? I mean—client—Rotherham—(*He tries a laugh*)—I mean, who'd go to Rotherham if it wasn't on *business*?

Clare Well that's a perfect start then. *You* go to Rotherham and I'll—I'll find something to amuse myself with *here.* Alone.

He eyes her suspiciously for a moment

George No, no—I don't think it's fair . . .

Clare Nonsense: of course you must go. It'll be a change for you. *And* me. Which is surely what we're talking about.

George (*after a moment*) Yes.

Clare After all, it's not as if we don't *trust* each other . . .

George Trust? What? Oh—yes—*absolutely.*

Clare Then we're agreed.

George Well, if you're . . .

Clare Yes, it's so obviously for the best. It was so clever of you to bring the matter up. I'll run your bath. (*She moves to the alcove then turns*) Do you know you only phoned me five times today?

George I *did* phone—this evening—but you were engaged.

Clare I don't . . . (*She remembers Nick's call*) Oh. *Yes.*

George Anyone important?

Clare Just a friend. No-one *you'd* know.

Clare exits

George watches her go suspiciously

George No-one *I* know? What does she . . .? Well if that's the way she feels . . . (*He moves to the telephone, carries it to the sofa, takes up a cushion as he dials. He puts the receiver to his ear, then holds the cushion against it in what he hopes will be sound-proofing*)

The bedsitter lights come up as he dials

Jane is about to get into bed. The telephone rings. She answers it

Jane Hello?

George (*quickly, furtively*) It's me—George.

Jane (*shooting a look at the alcove*) Yes?

George Lunch—tomorrow—well?

Jane Well, I . . .

Nick enters in his vest and pants. He pointedly ignores her

Fine.

Jane rings off. George rings off

Clare enters the drawing -room.

Jane gets into bed. Nick gets into bed, taking up his cigarettes and the ashtray. They sit up in bed, looking straight ahead

Clare I think I'll go to bed.

George Oh. Fine.

Clare moves to exit, but turns

Clare You've been having some very disturbed nights lately, George—
keeping me awake.
George Have I really? Sorry, darling.
Clare You wouldn't want me to sleep in the spare room.
George No, of course not, darling.

Again Clare almost exits and turns

And George—*do* stop stealing the ashtrays.

Clare exits

George stares after her

In the bedsitter, Nick pointedly flicks ash into the ashtray

CURTAIN

ACT II

SCENE 1

The same. Wednesday evening, two weeks later

Only the drawing-room is illuminated.

Clare enters, carrying a tray on which is a mound of sandwiches. She wears a new, seductive housecoat. She puts down the tray and crosses to put a chair at one end of the sofa. We should sense that it is a pretty wellworn routine by now. She is arranging subdued lighting when the doorbell rings. She quickly examines herself in the mirror and then exits, leaving the doors open. After a moment she re-enters, followed by Nick who wears his suit and has both hands behind his back. They come in and she closes the door

Nick Not too early, am I?

Clare Twenty-five to seven. Perfect.

Nick Only we *did* say half past six.

Clare That's what I mean—twenty-five to seven. Perfect.

Nick (*remembering he is the "doctor"*) Good. Good. For *you.* (*He withdraws a hand, produces a small bunch of flowers*)

Clare You shouldn't have . . . (*But in almost the same movement she is sticking them into an obviously-waiting pot*)

Nick For *us.* (*And he produces from behind his back a half-bottle of Spanish red*)

Clare Are you this generous with *all* your patients?

Nick There are patients and patients. (*Referring to the bottle*) Might I?

Clare Please.

She arranges herself on the sofa as Nick crosses to the drinks cabinet, fetches two glasses and the opener

Busy day?

Nick Exhausting. (*Starting to open the wine*) Apart from the clinic, there's my novel . . .

Clare You're writing a *novel.*

Nick My second. Based on personal experience, of course.

Clare Am *I* in it?

Nick (*with a professional chuckle*) Possibly—possibly . . . (*He pours two glasses, gives her one*) Cheers.

They drink. She restrains a grimace

Clare Delicious.

Nick One may not sympathize with their politics but one can hardly complain about their plonk. *Wine.*

Clare I agree: there's far too much snobbery about wine-drinking. After all, a grape's a grape whatever its political persuasion.

Nick True.

Clare Sandwich?

Nick Just a teeny bit peckish . . .

Clare Tell me, Nicholas.

Nick Yes.

Clare Do you believe in the stolen hour?

Nick Yes, yes I do.

Clare So much nicer than soggy cornflakes, don't you think?

Nick Pardon?

Clare That's what my husband's getting this weekend, you know.

Nick Is it?

Clare He's going away for the weekend (*Pointedly*) With a client.

Nick With a client?

Clare And we all know what that means don't we?

Clare moves to the radiogram and puts a smoochy record on

Nick The thing is—I think I should ring my colleague—just to make sure that George is all right . . .

He rises but she stops him and dances with him

Clare I don't care about George.

Nick Ah! You only *think* you don't care—in actual fact—you're exhibiting a typical psychological pattern.

Clare In actual fact. I'm *enjoying* myself.

Nick You only *think* you're enjoying yourself—on the surface you're calm—but inside—*inside* you're destroying yourself.

Clare Rubbish.

His mouth opens and closes

Nick But I'm an *expert*.

Clare You're also very young and very pretty.

She takes his hand. With his free hand he gulps down the wine

Nick (*brightly*) It's unethical.

Clare But you're a free man.

Nick Yes, but you're my patient.

Clare No, I'm not: my husband is.

Nick Doesn't that somehow make it *worse*?

Clare I think it makes it *lovely*.

Nick Does it? (*With doubt*) I could get struck off.

Clare Who'd tell? And you can't deny that we've grown very fond of each other over the past two weeks . . .

Nick Err . . .

Clare Well—while *he's* making free with this tart of his . . .

Nick starts to object but changes his mind

Nick You're right. Who does she think she is?

Clare A daughter-replacement figure.
Nick A what? Oh—yes—quite.
Clare Daughter-replacement figure. So if *he's* found a replacement figure—why shouldn't *I*?
Nick (*drinking more wine quickly*) You're right.
Clare You don't find me unattractive, do you Nicholas?
Nick No. *Me? What?* It's just that ... (*He gulps down more wine and blurts*) Psychiatrists have their problems too, you know.
Clare Tell me about them.

She takes his hand and guides him to the sofa. She pushes him into a lying position

The lights dim in the drawing-room and simultaneously come up in the bedsitter

George sits, trousers rolled up, bare feet in a bowl of water. A towel envelops his head: he's inhaling from a basin: quietly moaning miserably.

After a moment, Jane enters from the alcove, carrying a kettle. She looks at the heap that is George, sadly shakes her head, and crosses to pour water into the foot bowl

George (*at the heat*) Ahhh! (*He pulls the towel from his head, looks at her blearily, tries to smile, then speaks through his nose*) I think I've got a cold coming.
Jane (*with an edge*) I'll rub some Vick on your chest.
George (*brightening*) Would you really?
Jane (*flatly*) I haven't *got* any.
George Oh. I don't often get a cold, you know, but when I do Clare usually rubs Vick on the soles of my feet.
Jane The soles of your *feet*?
George Then I go to bed and the fumes rise.
Jane Wouldn't it have less distance to travel if she rubbed it on your chest.
George I've never thought about it. Anyway, it seems to work. *Clare* says ...
Jane I'm not interested in what *Clare* says.

Jane exits to the alcove with the kettle. We hear her banging around

George, realizing that she's annoyed, will make an effort. He takes his feet from the bowl and towels them

Jane enters

Jane I'm sorry.
George No—no—it's my fault—driving with the roof open.
Jane I didn't like to mention it. You seemed so pleased with your new toy. Car.
George I thought you'd *like* the roof open.
Jane A sunshine roof is for *sunshine*, George: not pouring rain.
George I couldn't shut it—it got jammed—it's so new, you see.

Jane Well let's hope it stops raining soon or I'll have to lend you an aqualung to drive home.

George Aqualung to drive home. I don't *often* get colds.

Jane Better now than next weekend.

George Yes.

A moment. Throughout the following, George folds the towel into a small, neat bundle

Jane You did book the tickets.

George (*nodding*) The twelve o'clock plane—Saturday.

Jane (*kissing his head*) It'll be marvellous.

George Yes.

Jane Paris. You don't think she'll . . .

George No. She thinks I'm in Rotherham.

Jane *Now?*

George No. On Saturday. I'll pick you up at about half past ten: we'll drive to the airport.

Jane If the car's dried out.

George "laughs" heartily and as he does his knees part and the towel falls down into the bowl of water.

Jane sighs and exits to the alcove

George lifts the soaking towel from the bowl, looks around for somewhere to put it, then sighs and drops it back into the bowl. He stands—still with trousers rolled up and bare-footed—and moves around, clearly not knowing what to do with himself. Suddenly he stops, stares, and then moves to take the ashtray (stolen by Nick) from the arm of the plastic chair. He stares at it—looks to the alcove—almost makes to ask Jane about it—but, still puzzled, puts the ashtray down again. Again he perambulates edgily for a moment

George What are we going to eat?

Jane (*off*) Oh— I meant to tell you.

Jane enters

I'm on a diet.

George Since when?

Jane This morning. It's fantastically healthy—will you have the same?

George Oh—yes—certainly. What sort of diet?

Jane Macrobiotic.

George That sounds—fantastic.

Jane It's what the Zen monks eat.

George Do they?

Jane It's all vegetables and rice.

George No meat?

Jane You see, according to the *monks*—food is divided into yin things and yang things.

George Oh really?
Jane We're eating yin.
George (*pointing to the floor*) Yin here? (*He "laughs"*).
Jane Yin *food. Vegetables.*
George No yang?
Jane Oh no—yang is *meat.* We mustn't eat *that.*

Jane exits

George I'd quite *like* some yang. (*He calls*) D'you want any help?
Jane (*off*) No, no—you just—take it easy.
George You don't want me to peel a carrot or anything?
Jane (*off*) No—no—you just relax.

George looks around, sighs, stuffs hands in pockets. Clearly the whole set-up is beginning to pall. He sees the telephone, glances towards the alcove, then quietly moves to bend down and take up the receiver

Jane enters

Immediately George slaps down the receiver and starts beating out a rhythm on the arm of the plastic chair, and whistling

How about some music?
George Lovely.
Jane (*sorting through her records*) Vivaldi?
George Oh. All right.
Jane What would you prefer.
George Have you anything by the Spew?
Jane The what?
George Spew.
Jane (*shaking her head*) No.
George Oh *yes*—the *Spew.*
Jane Are they in the charts?
George (*not understanding*) Certainly. They've just brought out a new singlet.
Jane What's it called?
George *You* know—*Peace on Earth and Goodwill To All Shipbuilders and Allied Building Trades.* (*He clicks his fingers. On every fifth click he moans "Peace"*)
Jane (*shaking her head*) No?

He stops. She puts a record on the turntable

This is the best I can do, I'm afraid.

A "Rolling Stones" record starts

George (*clicking his fingers*) Not bad—not bad . . . (*He starts to gyrate in what he fondly believes to be the modern idiom*)
Jane I'm not very fond of it myself. A friend must have left it. Excuse me.

Jane exits to the alcove

George alone gets bolder with his "dancing". He almost bumps into the bowl on the floor, bends to take it up—and his back locks solid. He stands, bent in half, hands clutching the bowl—can't move a muscle

George (*a pathetic plea*) Jane!

Jane appears in the alcove, looks at him

The lights dim in the bedsitter as the music stops and the drawing-room lights come up

Nick is lying on the sofa, knocking back a glass of scotch. Immediately Clare replenishes it from the bottle. She pours him a very large one. He drinks as she moves round to sit and stroke his head

Nick I'm a failure.
Clare Nonsense.
Nick 'Strue.
Clare What about your work?
Nick Work? Huh! (*He drinks*)
Clare Your *clinic*—all those people depending on you.
Nick Oh—them.
Clare And your *novel*.
Nick Oh—*that*.
Clare But surely that's wonderful in someone so young.
Nick (*momentarily brightening*) Did you know that I was an authority on The Use and Care of the Automatic Sewing Machine?
Clare Well there you *are* then. Have another.
Nick I couldn't
Clare Just a little one.

He raises his head to drink, which makes her "head-stroking" a little difficult so she changes tack and moves round to the other end of the sofa. She seductively removes his shoes, making great play of the laces, as he rambles on, apparently unaware of her activity

Nick Forget all the wonderful work I do. It's *me*—the human being. *That's* where I'm a failure. The thing is—I have never been properly loved. I was a bottle baby, you know.
Clare Oh dear: Phillip was a bottle baby.
Nick That's different: he had *you*.
Clare And so have *you*—now.
Nick It left me totally lacking in confidence. It's tragic when you think what an enormous potential I've got. Whatever I do goes wrong. You take girls. I can never keep one, you know. Of course—on the surface I appear to be in control—but underneath—underneath—I'm a blubbering heap.
Clare I can't believe it.
Nick 'Strue.

Clare (*stroking his brow*) All you need do is relax . . .

Clare pulls off one of his shoes in a gesture of finality—only to find that the sock has a large hole through which his toes protrude. She looks at the toes— he looks at the toes—then he reaches down to waggle them

Nick I *am* relaxed. This little piggy went to market, this little piggy stayed at home.

Clare And this little piggy had roast beef.

He struggles to sit up: she firmly pushes him down again then moves behind the sofa to switch off yet another light

Now close your eyes and think beautiful thoughts.

He closes his eyes. She leans over him

You're lying on a sun-drenched beach—golden sand—blue sea—waves gently lapping the shore—and someone is lying beside you—someone very close to your heart—who is it?

A moment. They both have their eyes closed. She's as caught up in the fantasy as he is

Nick Rodney Marsh.

Clare (*opening her eyes quickly*) Good. *Good.*

She kneels behind the sofa and strokes his brow. Eyes closed, he grins up happily

Now what you need—is someone—to look after you.

Nick I know it . . .

Clare Someone—who understands these things . . .

Nick (*drowsier*) I know it . . .

Clare Someone—mature.

Nick I know it . . .

Clare (*starting to unbutton his shirt*) I sometimes see myself as a glass of brandy——

He becomes aware of what she is doing, tries to sit up, but fails

—not perhaps a particularly fine example—but matured over good days—and not so bad nights—and definitely not to be taken lightly . . .

By now all the buttons are undone, and she opens the shirt and sees his vest

Mickey *Mouse?*

She stares down at him as he snores peacefully

The drawing-room lights fade as the bedsitter lights come up

George, on hands and knees, is being massaged by Jane. His shirt is tucked up to expose his bare back. He is still barefoot

George It's not as if I don't *love* her—I *do*—it's just that I'm not *in* love with her—d'you understand what I mean?

Jane Oh yes—I understand.

She digs her fingers in. He winces

George I mean—Clare (*he winces*)—she's been a wonderful—(*he winces*)—
wife—(*he winces*)—*wonderful.*
Jane Not hurting you, am I?
George (*bravely*) No, no.

She digs in deeper

I mean—let's face it—we've been married for twenty years—(*he winces*)
—I mean I'm *bound* to—you know . . .
Jane Oh yes—*I* know: I've got a father too.

Again she digs, he winces

I think that should do it.

She moves away. He gets up crookedly

Better?
George Much.

He tucks his shirt in, suddenly coy in her presence. She turns away helpfully

Anyway—we're all set for Saturday, then. (*He winces*)
Jane So it seems.
George We'll have—a lot of fun. (*He winces on trying to get into his coat*)
Jane A riot.
George I wonder if you'd mind . . .?

She helps him into his coat

Thank you.
Jane I suppose you're going now.
George Yes, I think I ought.
Jane Me too. I'll make you a warm drink.
George Thank you.

Jane exits to the alcove

George's nose starts to twitch. It builds into a huge sneeze

Jane appears in the alcove

Jane George.
George Yes Jane?
Jane (*flatly*) Why don't you wear a vest?

Jane exits. A moment, and then George exits miserably after her

The drawing-room lights come up

*Nick is doing up collar and tie. Clare sits, not looking at him, somehow
subdued*

Nick I'm terribly sorry: I can't think what came over me . . .
Clare (*more to herself*) Neither can I.
Nick It must be all this work—clinic—novel—sewing machines . . . (*with a sudden bright thought*) You don't think I'm heading for a nervous breakdown, do you?
Clare (*standing*) Nick . . .
Nick Yes Clare?
Clare It's me who should be sorry.
Nick What for?
Clare (*smiling slightly, shaking head*) It doesn't matter. (*She moves to open the door*)
Nick Clare?
Clare Yes?
Nick (*moving to her*) Same time next week?
Clare I'm—not sure. Perhaps you should give me a ring.

Nick and Clare exit

Jane and George enter through the alcove. He is fully dressed now. She takes down his hat, hands it to him

George Until Saturday then.
Jane (*rather flatly*) Yes.
George Unless—lunch—tomorrow?
Jane Perhaps you'd better stay in bed—get rid of that cold.
George (*after a moment*) Yes. Well then . . .

There is a tiny awkward pause. He bends to kiss her

Best not. You know—*germs*.
Jane Yes.

She opens the door. He moves out. They flutter fingers at each other

George Saturday then.
Jane Saturday.

A moment. Then he moves out of sight. She almost closes the door, but calls after him

Don't forget to tell Clare to rub some Vick on your feet.

George exits

Jane closes the door. She sighs, suddenly looking very miserable. She moves away from the door

Clare enters the drawing-room

At the same time, Clare and Jane each take up a newspaper, move to sit, open the newspaper to read. As they do this we hear the sound of a car starting.

Jane reacts slightly to this. Then we hear the sound of a short but noisy, brake-squealing journey. The car stops—a door slams. Clare reacts slightly to this. There is a moment's pause

> *George enters the drawing-room and, at the same time, Nick enters the bedsitter*

The women, behind their newspapers, ignore them. It's clear that all four want to make some sort of peace but don't know how to begin. Silence

George I think I've got a cold coming.
Nick I fell asleep tonight.
Clare You'd better have a hot bath.
Jane Go to bed.

George ⎫ Yes. ⎰ *Speaking*
Nick   ⎭   ⎱ *together*

Pause

George I couldn't close the roof of my car.
Nick I think I've been over-working.
Clare I'll bring you up a hot drink.
Jane I think there's some milk left.
George If it's—no trouble.
Nick You don't mind?

Clare ⎫ No, no. ⎰ *Speaking*
Jane ⎭   ⎱ *together*

George and Nick move away

Clare ⎫ George ... ⎰ *Speaking*
Jane ⎭ Nick ...   ⎱ *together*

The men turn

Clare (*shaking her head slightly*) It doesn't matter.
Jane Nothing.

The men move back

George ⎫ I've been thinking ... ⎰ *Speaking*
Nick   ⎭   ⎱ *together*
Clare Yes?
Jane What about?
George About our—arrangement.
Nick Our relationship.
Clare What about it?
Jane I didn't think you cared.
George You still want to go ahead.
Nick Me?
Clare If *you* want to.
Jane It's you who spoiled it.

George It was your idea.
Nick It isn't.
Clare It wasn't.
Jane ⎱
George ⎰ Then who *was* it? ⎰ *Speaking*
                                    ⎱ *together*
Nick ⎱
Clare ⎰ *You.* ⎰ *Speaking*
                    ⎱ *together*
Jane ⎱
George ⎰ *Me?* ⎰ *Speaking*
                    ⎱ *together*
Nick ⎱
Clare ⎰ Yes! ⎰ *Speaking*
                  ⎱ *together*
Jane You asked for it.
George ⎱
Nick ⎰ How? ⎰ *Speaking*
                 ⎱ *together*
Clare The way you've been behaving.
Jane You're totally irresponsible.
George Charming.
Nick Typical.
Clare Not altogether.
Jane *Yes.*
George At least you could have met me halfway.
Nick Well that's *me.*
Clare And admit it was all *my* fault.
Jane Abso-bloody-lutely.
George Well that *does* it.
Nick I'm glad you understand.
Clare You can please yourself.
Jane I do.
George I will.
Nick *Fine.*
Clare *Excellent.*

The two men sit, simultaneously, with an air of aggressive finality. Pause

Jane I'm going away this weekend.
George It's all arranged you know.
Nick Good.
Clare What is?
Jane Paris.
George Rotherham.
Nick Oh yes—your sugar-daddy.
Clare Of course—your client.
Jane He's picking me up—*here.*
George Saturday morning—definitely.
Nick Excellent.
Clare Fine.

A moment. Then George and Jane rise, make to exit. George takes up the half bottle of wine

George Have you been slumming?
Clare Snob.

George exits

Jane You'll never be *half* the man your mother was!

Jane exits to the alcove

For a moment, Nick and Clare remain, fuming. Then both make up their minds . . . Clare moves quickly to dial the telephone as Nick pulls out his little address book to search for her number. He is just about to take up the telephone when it rings. He snatches it up

Nick (*in an irritable shout*) Hello!
Clare Hello! Are you *doing* anything this weekend?

George and Jane enter

Nick and Clare turn to look at them, smiling flatly. Then, as they turn their attention back to the telephone, the light fades to a Black-Out.

SCENE 2

The same. The following Saturday morning.

The lights come up on the bedsitter.

Jane, in bra and pants, is packing a suitcase with frillies. Nick is standing on his head on the floor, his feet against the wall

Jane (*after a moment*) You've been doing that all morning.
Nick I'm fighting off tooth decay.
Jane He's coming here, you know.
Nick Don't worry: I'll be out of the way.
Jane Not there you won't.
Nick Actually—I'm thinking.
Jane About not going? Not a chance.
Nick About *her.*
Jane *Who* her?
Nick That—woman I was telling you about. The one I met at the group the other night. I think I might give her a ring.
Jane Where—at the Old Age Pensioners' Club?
Nick (*ignoring this*) Theatre—dinner—spot of wine—know what I mean?
Jane Oh yes, *I* know what you mean—front row at the Roxy—fish and chips—half a bottle of Spanish plonk—now let me see—that should come to about one pound twenty. Would you like it *now*—or is *she* paying?
Nick (*still ignoring*) Maybe back to *her* place—few more drinks—lights

down low—boom-boom—(*with a sudden thought*)—or maybe even bring her back *here*.

Jane Why not? Boom-boom.

Nick (*getting up*) Yeah that's a very good idea, why not? (*He moves to the door*)

Jane I won't change my mind, you know.

Nick ("*smiling*") Don't forget your curlers.

Nick exits

The bedsitter lights fade and the drawing-room lights come up

Clare is Hoovering the carpet

George enters, minus jacket, carrying a pair of bright pyjamas. He puts them in a suitcase. Clare ignores him. He almost exits, but changes his mind and moves to speak to her with incredible formality

George Excuse me . . .

Clare ignores him and starts to tra-la-la gaily

Excuse me.

She sings louder. He crosses and turns off the Hoover at the wall-plug

Where are my vests?

Clare I've used them.

George *Used* them? What for?

Clare Dusters.

George *Dusters?*

Clare You told me to get rid of them.

George I meant put them away.

Clare For a rainy day?

George Ha!

She pulls out a duster and dabs at a table. George makes to exit

Clare Anyway—I thought you didn't *wear* vests any more.

George I wear vests—when I *choose* to wear vests.

Clare Oh well, in that case I'll put this in your drawer for you. (*She holds up the duster in both hands to reveal that it is a stained and holey vest*)

George exits

Clare carries on polishing

George enters with a handful of aerosol sprays, men's toiletries. He stuffs them in the case, but pointedly gives a great squirt with one of the sprays, then sniffs, satisfied

Won't that lacquer sting your bald patch?

George I do not *have* a bald patch.

Clare Anyway, I shouldn't use it, George: not *hair* lacquer. It's like sleep-with a Brillo Pad. (*He ignores her and tries to get the lid of the case closed. It proves a difficult task*)

(*Winding up the Hoover lead*) Will you be going in your new car?

George Naturally.

Clare Ah.

George Ah what?

Clare I thought you might have hired a Landrover.

George And why should I want to hire a Landrover pray?

Clare To carry all your medical supplies.

George I sometimes suffer from a slight chest: I always *have*.

Clare Yes, I remember your mother used to wrap you in brown paper.

George It didn't stop me playing stand-off half for my county.

Clare Or driving your new car. Broom-broom.

George *Should* I suffer a relapse this weekend—which is most unlikely—I've no doubt that I shall be able to make myself perfectly well understood in the local—pharmaceutery.

Clare Yes: I understand they speak quite good English in Rotherham.

He almost answers, but checks himself and resumes struggling with the case

George Would you mind sitting on my case?

Clare I haven't the time. (*She moves towards the alcove with the Hoover*)

George Where are you going?

Clare To the hairdressers.

George What for?

Clare To have my hair done.

George Why?

Clare Because it needs it. Well I thought while you're in Rotherham—I might go into town—you never know—*meet* someone.

George There's still *time* you know.

Clare Absolutely.

George No, no, no . . . there's still time for me to cancel my trip.

Clare And ruin your client's weekend (*At the alcove*) Nonsense, George. In case you've gone when I get back—do write, even if it's only a cheque.

Clare exits, followed by George with the suitcase

The lights fade in drawing room and come up in bedsitter

The doorbell rings in the bedsitter

Jane starts, looks at her watch, and then pulls on her housecoat and opens the door

Jack Bowers enters. At fifty, he wears clothes for someone at least half his age

Jane Good God.
Jack Hello, Janey.

Throughout the following, for all his surface flash, we should sense a sad man. And it is important that Jane should be just that little too brittle: it's a thin and painful veneer

Can I come in?
Jane Why not?

She opens the door wider. He comes in, looking around. She closes the door, looks at him

And what do I owe the pleasure? You aren't due for another five years.
Jack (*trying a "grin"*) You sound more like your mother every time I see you.
Jane Which, let's face it, isn't very often.
Jack It hasn't been easy since the divorce.
Jane You look as if you've suffered.
Jack I mean *you. Me.*
Jane How did you track me down?
Jack Your mother gave me your address.
Jane (*flatly*) Good old mum.
Jack I see from the nameplate downstairs you're using her name.
Jane I'm on *her* side, remember?
Jack Which is why I've stayed out of your way.
Jane Oh yes. "Consideration" was always your middle name. "Never" was your *first.*

He looks at her, but then moves away, points to the suitcase

Jack Going somewhere?
Jane That's right. For the weekend. (*She looks at her watch*) Very soon as a matter of fact.
Jack I just thought—you—know—I'd—drop by—see how you were making out.
Jane Thanks. *Dad.*

A moment

Jack Well—I'll be off then. (*He looks at her, moves to door*)
Jane Look—you don't *have* to go—I'm going to have a shower—why don't you—I don't know—make a cup of coffee or something.
Jack (*moving back*) Well if you're . . .
Jane Yes.

A moment

Jack Thanks, Janey.

Jane moves to the alcove; turns. He has his back to her. And in this moment, we see beneath her veneer. She almost says something, but changes her mind

Jane exits

Jack looks around, moves to sit at the foot of the bed

The door opens and Nick comes in. He stops dead at seeing Jack

Nick Oh. *You're* here, are you?
Jack (*standing*) Yes.
Nick Where's Jane?
Jack Having a shower.

Nick moves to him

Nick (*confidentially*) It was bound to happen.
Jack What?
Nick Us meeting.
Jack Was it?
Nick 'Course—she hasn't *told* you about *me*.
Jack No.
Nick (*smirking*) So now you know.
Jack Yes. (*But clearly he does not*)
Nick I've know all about *you* from the word go.
Jack I—somehow didn't think she'd talk about me.
Nick What? Oh yes—I know all about *you*, mate: you're just a dirty old
    man.
Jack (*with a wry chuckle*) Is that what she calls me?
Nick Not *her*, mate: *me*. (*Quietly*) I'd better go—if she found out I'd met
    you, she'd have a fit. (*He gets on his knees and drags a tatty suitcase from
    under the bed, then gets up*) You'd better not say anything about seeing
    me—for her sake. Does that surprise you?
Jack Well, I . . .
Nick I *worry* about her, you know—not that *she* cares.
Jack Who *are* you?
Nick Me? I'm her psychiatrist.
Jack Her what?
Nick Psychiatrist. She's one of my cases. (*He holds up the suitcase*) This is
    another one. (*He moves to the door, but returns, unable to resist*) I know
    exactly what she's going through. It's just a stage. She'll come round—
    you see. Enjoy your weekend.
Jack Thanks.
Nick And remember—for *her* sake . . . (*With a finger to his lips*) Sssh.
    (*He moves to the door, opens it, then turns*) You're just a father-figure
    to *her*, cock.

Nick exits

Jack sits on the bed, trying to work it out

Jane enters, pulling on a dress

Jane (*turning her back to him and referring to the zip*) Please.

He zips her up

Jack You're all right—are you Janey?

Jane (*moving to the mirror*) How do you mean—all right?

Jack You know—your—personal life.

Jane Fine.

Jack Only I wouldn't want to think that what happened between—me and your mother—has left any sort of —well—*scar*.

Jane Oh but it *has*—according to my psychiatrist.

Jack (*tentatively*) You—*have* got a psychiatrist.

Jane A *personal* one: tends me night and day.

Jack What exactly does he—say?

Jane He says that all I want is a father-figure: let's face it, I've never *had* one. Not like *this* one, anway.

Jack (*worried*) What one?

Jane (*brightly*) Didn't I say? I'm going away with him this weekend. He's just about *your* age, as a matter of fact.

Jack (*sitting on the bed*) Janey—you're making a terrible mistake.

Jane So I'm told.

Jack It won't work. If anyone should know, it's me.

Jane Oh yes: how *is* your little model-stroke-actress?

Jack Look—I'm only down for the weekend—why don't you spend it with *me*—we can talk . . .

Jane "Get to know each other" is, I think, the usual terminology.

Jack *Please.*

Jane Sorry. Too late. Much. (*With a change of tone*) If only you'd *said* you were coming.

Jack (*smiling*) I know. (*He looks at her for a moment, then reaches into a pocket to pull out a card*) If you change your mind—'phone me at my hotel . . .

(*She takes the card, looks at it, and suddenly throws her arms about his neck*)

Jane Oh, *Daddy* . . .

They cling to each other for a moment. Then he breaks away, smiles, moves to the door, opens it, then turns

Jack You know, Janey—the devil of it is—if I had my life to live all over again, I'd make the same mistakes. Only I'd probably make them sooner.

Jack exits

Jane stands looking into the mirror. She feels awful. She almost makes to go after him but, forcing it to the back of her mind, goes to the alcove

Jane exits

The lights come up in the drawing-room

George enters from the french windows. His sleeves are rolled up, his arms black with grease. He holds an oily rag and the large air filter to a carburettor

George Bloody *car* . . . (*He glares around, trying to think what to do with the air filter*)

The telephone rings. George is stuck with the filter and oily rag, dare not put them down, holds them in one hand and picks up the receiver delicately between two fingers

(*Bad tempered*) *Hello* . . . (*He listens, and brightens suddenly*) Jack. You what? Lunch? Oh my . . . No of course I didn't forget . . . No, no, she's looking forward to seeing you—hasn't stopped talking about it. Good old Jack, she keeps saying . . . *Great* . . . By taxi? . . . About—what—twenty minutes . . . No, no – come straight over. I'll have a scrum half's special waiting on the touch-line . . . That's the one—whisky, rum, vodka and a splash of petrol. *Great.* (*He rings off, delighted*) Good old *Jack.* (*He looks down at the air filter, moves across and tosses it out of the french windows, moves to the doors, wiping his hands on the rag*) Clare? (*He waits a moment. Then, satisfied that she isn't in, hurries to the telephone and dials, cheerily starting to sing one of his awful rugby club songs*)

The telephone rings out in the bedsitter

Jane enters from the alcove to answer it

Jane Hello?
George Jane? It's *me.*

Jane closes her eyes, willing him to say the right thing

Jane Yes?
George About this weekend——
Jane You can't make it . . .
George —something's just cropped up . . .
Jane Oh dear.
George Are you *terribly* disappointed?
Jane Terribly.
George There'll be other times.
Jane Next week.
George *Definitely.*
Jane I'll wait to hear from you then.
George Soon.
Jane Miss you.
George You too.

They blow kisses and simultaneously ring off. Both obviously very happy and relieved. George whistles his way across to the drinks cabinet, dropping the rag en route, and checks the contents, Jane stands for a moment. Then takes up the card left by her father. A moment. Then she dials the telephone

Jane (*after a moment*) Winchelsea Hotel? (*She turns her back, so that we do not see or hear her speak*)

Clare enters the drawing-room, with a new hairdo

Clare Haven't you gone yet?
George I'm not going.
Clare (*shocked*) Why?
George *Jack.*
Clare *Jack?*
George It's the fourteenth. He's coming for lunch. You put it in your *diary.*
Clare I forgot.
George (*shaking his head*) Clare. (*He "tut-tuts"*)
Clare He can't come.
George He's on his way.
Clare But your business trip.
George I've put it off.
Clare What *for?*
George *Jack.* Good old *Jack!* (*He holds up a bottle*) Must get some booze. (*Moving to her*) You look terrific. Give us a kiss.

George kisses Clare briefly, savours her lipstick with relish, and exits happily through the french windows

Clare stands, stunned, Then she hurries to the telephone, and dials

Jane (*into the receiver*) I'll see you later then. 'Bye.

Jane hangs up, and immediately it rings again. She takes it up

Hello?
Clare I must speak to Doctor Nicholas Craig.
Jane Doctor . . . ? He isn't *here.*
Clare You mean he's already left?
Jane So it seems.
Clare Then I'm too late.
Jane Are you?
Clare Yes. (*She hangs up*)

Jane shrugs, hangs up. Clare stands staring down at the telephone. The house doorbell rings

Clare starts, stares at the door, then hurries out. Jane collects up her coat and goes out of the bedsitter

The bedsitter lights dim

Ruth is ushered in by Clare

I thought you were *him*.
Ruth Who?
Clare It's all your fault.
Ruth *What* is?
Clare I should have written to Anna Raeburn.

The doorbell rings

You *see?*
Ruth What?
Clare I've got to get rid of him.

Clare exits hurriedly

Ruth shrugs, moves into the room, notices the rag left by George, picks it up between two fingers and deposits it outside the french windows

Clare enters, followed by a smiling Jack

Ruth Jack Jack Ruth.

Ruth and Jack shake hands

Ruth Oh, so *you're* Jack.
Clare (*worried stiff*) I just *said* that, didn't I?
Jack George been talking about me, has he?
Ruth Never stops.

Jack and Ruth have clearly taken an instant liking to each other

You must tell me about the time you nearly scored a try against the Barbarians ...
Clare He will—he will—I *know* he will ...

George enters through the french windows, gay as a lark, carrying an off-licence box stacked high

George Hello Ruth—how *nice* to see you!

He kisses Ruth on the cheek. She stares at him. He sees Jack

Jack!
Jack George!

George puts down the box as Jack moves to him. George snatches a large bag of crisps from the box and tosses it to Jack, like a rugby ball. They go through a bit of rugby playing mime (scrum half to fly half passes) finishing with a couple of lines from a rugby club song

Ruth I'd better be going.
George Nonsense! Stay and have lunch.
Ruth Pardon?

George Lunch. (*He puts an arm around her shoulders*) Make up the four.
Jack Look—it's a terrible liberty, George—but I've asked my daughter
to come over—I haven't seen her since she moved down here—and I
knew you wouldn't . . .
George Of *course* we wouldn't mind—*love* to meet her, wouldn't we, Clare?
Clare (*still worried stiff*) Love to.

George starts to pour drinks

George Tell you what. Stay the weekend. (*He puts an arm round Clare*) It'll
be great fun, won't it, darling?
Clare (*flatly*) Great fun.
Jack Are you sure . . .?
George Don't worry about a thing. Clare's a wonderful organizer, aren't
you, darling?
Clare Incredible. (*Suddenly*) *Drinks.*
George Just doing it.

*Clare points dramatically towards the french windows and moves towards
Ruth*

Clare In the garden. Everyone down to the bottom of the garden for
drinks. *Now.*
Ruth (*sensing something*) Yes, come along, Jack. (*She links arms with
Jack*) I'll show you where George is having his new sauna bath.

Ruth guides Jack through the french windows

Clare George. I must speak to you.
George I know exactly what you're going to say.
Clare You do?
George And you're absolutely right.
Clare I am?
George Absolutely. I mean, it's obvious. Just you and me in this great
big house. That's obviously been the trouble. We needed *company*.
Clare Not all at once.
George It was all my fault.
Clare No, no—I'm just as much to blame . . .
George No, no. *My* fault. Anyway—all over now.
Clare Not quite.
George (*with full magnanimity*) Yes. I *forgive* you.
Clare No matter what?
George No matter what. (*He carries a trayful of drinks with dishes of nuts,
pretzels etc., towards the french windows*)
Clare I hope you remember that, George.

George continues on his way

George . . .

George turns

Ask Ruth to pop in for a minute, will you?
George *Certainly.*

George exits to the terrace

(Off, calling) Ruthikins!

Clare stares after him then swallows a large drink

Ruth enters with a glass

Ruth He really is rather *nice.*
Clare Who?
Ruth *Jack.*
Clare Don't worry about Jack—worry about *Nick.*
Ruth Nick? Oh—*Nick.*
Clare He's coming here—for the weekend.
Ruth Why?
Clare Because *I* asked him.
Ruth *(shrugging)* Well that seems as good a reason as any . . .
Clare I thought George was going *away.*
Ruth Oh—I *see.*
Clare No, you don't!

The doorbell rings

It's *him:* what can I do?
Ruth Well—he's your husband's psychiatrist, isn't he?
Clare Yes.
Ruth Then say he just—popped in. With some pills or something.
Clare But he's got so *many* pills.

The doorbell rings again

Help me, Ruth.
Ruth What can *I* do?
Clare Get rid of him. Say—say I'm cooking the lunch —dinner—*anything.*

Clare hurriedly exits. Ruth shrugs and exits after her. George enters from the french windows. He crosses to the drinks cabinet and collects the ice-bucket

George *(shouting)* What was the name of that fella who had his ear bitten off?
Jack *(off; shouting)* What fella who had his ear bitten off?
George *(shouting)* You know—thingy—the one who had his ear bitten off.
Jack *(off; shouting)* Oh—Paddy McGonagle.
George *(shouting, as he starts to exit)* Paddy McGonagle! No, Paddy's was the right ear—I'm talking about the fella who couldn't find his left ear . . .

George takes the ice-bucket with him as he exits through the french windows

Ruth enters followed by Jane

Jane I hope it's all right: Daddy just gave me the address and told me to come on.

Ruth They'll be delighted, I know they will. Have you met them?

Jane Once. I was about three, I think.

Ruth You'll like them. I'll just go and tell Mrs Williams you're here . . . (*She moves, then stops*) Tell you what—the men are reliving their youth at the bottom of the garden—why don't you pour yourself a drink and then join them?

Jane (*smiles*) Thanks.

Ruth exits

Jane looks around and moves towards the drinks cabinet

George enters through the french windows singing a snatch of a rugby song. He waves cheerily at Jane as he comes. Then suddenly he stops—stares— the words dying away on his lips

Mister—Williams?

He slowly nods

George *Jane?*

She nods

Jane *Daddy's*—Mister Williams?

George *Daddy's?*

Jack enters breezily through the french windows

Jack That was never a forward pass, you know . . . never in a million years . . . (*He sees Jane and moves to her, kisses her, puts an arm around her*) Janey darling, bless you . . .

Jane (*still staring at George*) It was—nothing.

Jack You two have met then.

George ⎱ No. Yes. ⎰ *Speaking*
Jane ⎰   ⎱ *together*

Jack Didn't think she'd turn out like this, did we George?

George (*shaking his head weakly*) No.

Jack (*kissing her cheek*) How old were you—three?

George Three?

Jack And *now* look at her.

George I am.

Clare and Ruth enter

Jack Ah! Clare—this is my little Janey—sorry—*Jane.*

Clare Hello, Jane.

Jack You won't remember Clare of course, Janey.

Jane No: but I feel I know a great deal about her—one way and another.

George gives a sudden blurt of "laughter". Everyone looks at him

Jack And this is Ruth.

George Yes — All that's Ruth.

Ruth Yes — we've already met. (*She smiles*)

Jack (*jokingly, behind his hand*) *Auntie* Ruth of the *Woman's Gazette*. You might have written to her.

Jane No: but I think I might soon.

The doorbell rings

George Who the hell's that?

Clare (*blurts*) Ruth . . .

George Ruth?

Clare *Ruth's* friend.

George She hasn't got any friends.

Ruth *What?*

Clare Your friend—*friend*—you asked him for *lunch—remember?*

Jack Oh: there's a pity.

Ruth (*more to Clare*) Just—an acquaintance really.

Clare Yes. You *will* be surprised when you meet him, George. I must go and lunch the cook—er—cook the lunch.

Clare exits

George But we haven't got one.

Ruth exits after Clare

The doorbell rings again

Let me show you the garden—there's grass—green grass . . . (*He grabs Jane and manoeuvres her towards the french windows*)

Jack Isn't anyone going to answer the door?

George Someone will—I *know* they will . . .

Jane and George exit to the garden. Jack shrugs and moves to the french windows. He "hovers" outside.
Ruth enters, followed by Nick who carries his suitcase and flowers and wears a worried expression

Ruth (*as she enters*) Don't worry, you're with me.

Nick With you?

Ruth The thing is—(*quietly*)—her husband hasn't gone away.

Nick Oh. (*Realizing*) *What?* But why didn't she tell me?

Ruth Apparently she *did* phone—but your nurse said you'd already left.

Nick Nurse?

Jack enters with glass in hand, "casually" through the french windows

Nick instantly shoves the flowers at Ruth

Jack Soda.
Nick For *you*.
Ruth (*to Jack*) This is Nicholas.
Jack (*surprised*) We've already met.
Ruth Have you?
Nick Oh yes. We've met. Yes. Oh *yes*.
Ruth Well—there's a surprise. Well—if you'll excuse me, I'll—er—
   (*squeezing Nick's arm*)—just go and tell Clare that everything's *all right*.
Nick Fine. Good. Yes.

Ruth exits with the flowers

   (*Aggressive*) I thought you were going to Paris.
Jack (*shaking his head, not understanding*) Bradford.
Nick She said *Paris*.
Jack Who?
Nick *Jane*.
Jack No—Bradford. Monday.

Nick suddenly realizes he's holding a suitcase. He puts it down

Nick (*referring to the case*) I'm not staying.

George enters from the french windows, followed by Jane

George How can I be expected to remember someone when the last time
   I saw them they were *three*.

*George crosses straight to the drinks table. Jane sees Nick. They both react.
She makes to exit quickly to the french windows but Nick grabs her*

Nick What are you doing *here*?
Jane What are *you* doing here?
Nick You were supposed to be going *away* for the weekend.
Jane I changed my mind.
Nick Why come *here*?
Jane I came with my father if you must know.

Nick looks at George and goes to shake his hand

Nick How d'you do?
George (*still dazed*) How d'you do.
Nick (*to Jack, realizing*) You mean you came *here*?
Jack We're old friends.
George Do you two know each other?
Jane (*quickly*) No.
Jack (*to Nick*) But you're her psychiatrist.
Jane My *psychiatrist*?

Clare and Ruth enter

Clare (*over brightly*) Isn't it *incredible*—Ruth's friend being my husband's psychiatrist?
George (*staring*) Incredible.
Jack Everyone you meet now seems to be going to a psychiatrist nowadays.
Nick (*to Jack*) *Don't* they? (*He draws a hand across his throat*)

Jack stares at him

Jane (*very pointedly*) Ruth's *friend*.
Clare Nicholas. (*To Nick*) Of course, we've never met, have we, Nick?
Nick (*shaking his head*) Never. (*Suddenly*) *Ruth?* Who's Ruth?
Ruth (*putting an arm in his*) *Me*, darling.
Nick Oh yes—so you are (*He smiles weakly*)
Jane (*still very pointedly*) So *you're* his friend.
Ruth (*smiling*) Acquaintance.
Jane So I *hear*.
Clare (*still overbrightly*) Lunch won't be long.
Jack (*putting an arm around Clare*) Fantastic cook, this little lady. (*He kisses her*)
Nick (*quickly*) Is she? Is she really?
Clare Why don't we all sit down?

George bends to guide Ruth into a chair. In doing so, he backs into Nick. George backs away and makes to sit in another chair but Nick is about to sit in the same one and George finds himself bumped away again. So—Jane and Jack sit on the sofa—Ruth and Nick sit on chairs. Clare takes George's arm and guides him towards the french windows

(*Brightly*) Can you spare me a moment?

George and Clare stand near the french windows

(*In a "whisper"*) I found out.

George Found out?
Clare About you seeing a psychiatrist.
George Me?
Clare Every Wednesday.
George Oh. Yes.

Clare exits through the french windows

George stares from her to the others then "laughs" merrily

That was a good one! (*He continues to "laugh" as the others stare at him. He moves to the middle of the room and surveys them all*) Well—isn't this *nice?*
Nick I wonder what the *weather's* like.
Jack Looks pretty good to me.
Nick In *Paris.*
Jack Drizzle.
Nick Oh, you checked up, did you?

Jack (*cheerily*) That's me: I've always had an interest in the weather.
Nick (*to Jane*) That's him—wet and windy.

Clare enters with the drinks tray and constantly moves around, distributing drinks, nuts, pretzels, etc., during the following

Jane (*with an edge*) So you're Auntie Ruth?
Clare And Sister Goodheart.
George And Madame Zenda.
Jane I was going to *write* to you.
George (*worried*) Were you?
Jane Yes.
George What about.
Jane (*to Ruth*) About this friend of mine.
Ruth The inevitable friend (*She smiles*)
Jane A man.
George *Man?*
Jane *Youth*, actually.
George (*relieved*) Yes—youth. A very *young* youth.
Ruth Fire away.
Clare (*proferring her tray*) Nut, anyone?
George Perhaps Auntie Ruth doesn't want to talk shop.
Ruth Oh, I don't mind: It's all in a days work. Don't *you* find that, Nick?
Nick Me? Work? Oh—*yes*. Work, work, work. Never stops.
Jane Never *starts*.
Jack *I* knew a psychiatrist once . . .
Nick *Careful.*
Clare Psychiatry works wonders. (*To George*) Doesn't it?
George (*looking at Nick*) Miracles.
Jane (*firmly*) This *friend*——
George (*anxiously*) *Youth.* You'll remember he's a *youth* . . .
Jane —this *friend* is apparently besotted with a woman old enough to be his *grandmother*.
Jack (*brightly*) Perhaps he likes antiques.
Nick I'd be very careful If I were you.
Jack Eh?
Nick (*advancing menacingly on him*) *Bradford.*
Ruth I *like* Bradford.
Nick Pity it hasn't got an Eiffel *Tower.*
Clare (*helpfully*) Blackpool has.
Jack Went dancing at the Blackpool Tower once.
Nick You're quite the little mover from what I hear.

George changes the subject and points dramatically at Jack

George This man had the best pair of hands in the business. (*He mimes passing a rugby ball*)
Nick Pity he couldn't keep them to himself. (*He mimes passing the ball back again*)
Jack What is it about me?

Jane (*taking his hand*) You're *lovely*.

Jack kisses her cheek. Nick looks disgusted

Clare (*proferring her tray*) Nut, anyone?
Jane Well—what do you think—about this friend of mine?
George Pity he isn't here to speak for himself. (*He "laughs"*)
Jack Anyway, the Eiffel Tower's in *Paris*.
Nick *I* have a very similar case at the moment—sensitive—creative—intelligent—we *all* know what *he's* seeking.
Clare (*proferring her tray*) Gherkin?
Nick Understanding. (*He grabs a gherkin*) Someone to recognize his—his—
Clare —enormous potential?
George (*shocked*) *Clare* darling.
Jane Like Rodney Marsh Hairgrips.
Ruth *Rodney*, dear.
Nick (*delightedly*) Do you *know* Rodney?
Jack *I* met Bobby Charlton.
Clare In the shower?
George Does wonders with his *hair*.
Ruth Who?
George Bobby Charlton.
Nick Let's not talk about *him*—(*To Jack*) let's talk about *you*.
Ruth (*lightly*) What is this—a group therapy session?
Clare My husband has *those*.
Nick (*to Jack, pointedly*) Every *Wednesday*.
George (*nodding, looking at Jane*) Yes.
Jane I still want to know what you think about this friend of mine.
Ruth All right—how old is he—about—what—Nick's age?
Clare (*worried*) Oh no—I shouldn't think so.
Jane Yes.
Ruth Then why don't we play a little game?
George (*worried*) What sort of game?
Ruth Don't worry, darling: nothing energetic.
Jack What's it called?
Ruth Let's pretend.
George Let's pretend *what*?
Ruth Well—for a start—let's say that Nick is this friend of Jane's.
Jack (*brightly catching on*) Oh—it's a *game*!
Nick Yes! You should enjoy it. All right, I'm him.
Ruth Now we've all heard *your* side of the problem: frustration. Where could *that* have started?
Clare (*proferring her tray*) Bottle-baby, anyone?
Nick (*playing the "game"*) I've got this *girl friend*. She inhibits my dynamic thrust.
George I say, old boy—steady on . . .
Ruth Right. Girl-friend. (*To Jane*) Say someone of *your* age, Jane. Now why would she do *that*?
Jane Because the only dynamic thrusting *he* does is into *my* handbag.
Nick Rubbish.
Jane And no sense of responsibility.

Ruth And how do you get back at him?
Nick She finds herself a sugar-daddy, that's *how*.
Ruth Sugar-daddy. That's *you* . . . (*She jabs George in the rump*)
George Me?
Nick (*pointing to Jack*) Why not *him*?
Jack Me?
Ruth (*to George*) Why does a married man like *you* go with a girl of *her* age?

George splutters

George Why don't you ask *her* why someone of her age goes with a married man of *my* age?
Jane Because married men are so *grateful*.
Jack (*ruefully*) Very true.

Nick reacts in amazement

George Oh I *see—grateful*, is it? The only reason a decent upright married man like—*him*—would go with a girl like *her*—is because she *flaunted* herself at him—deliberately left her umbrella at home.
Jane She did not *flaunt* herself—she was touched by his stories about his boring old wife—he was so *pathetic*.
George He is *not* pathetic!
Nick (*at Jack*) *I* think he is.
Jack What *is* it about me?
Ruth Right. Wife. How old would *she* be?
Clare (*quickly*) About *your* age, I should think.
Jane Fifty?

George roars with nervous laughter. They all look at him

George That's a bit *strong* isn't it?
Jane Why? (*At Ruth, sweetly*) It's only a game.
George Yes of course it is—a game . . .
Ruth That's right, *dear*—just a game. I'm the wife then. And *I* know what my husband's going through because it happens to *all* men of his age.
Clare It's called the Virility Crisis.
George My god, that sounds *terrible*.
Nick It *is*. (*Referring to Jack*) Ask *him*. Better still, *look* at him.

Jack looks down at himself, bewildered. Jane takes his arm

Jane I suppose she read about it in one of your articles.
Clare I never read her articles. (*To Ruth*) I mean—*did* you?
Ruth No—I asked a friend.
George And what did this friend *say?*
Ruth Ask her. (*She points at Clare*)
Clare Me?
Ruth You're the pretend friend.
Clare Oh. I—er—I said she should stoke up the bath and top up the fire.
George She sounds like a maid in some country hotel.
Jack Oh—we're in a *hotel*.

George No, no, no . . .

Clare Well you see—after twenty years, the water gets cold.

Nick (*at Jack*) And *dirty.*

George What did she say—this *friend?*

Clare I said—I said . . .

Ruth *She* said—being a woman of some experience—let them see *more* of each other.

Jack (*totally confused*) Who?

Ruth (*pointing to Jane and George*) Him and her.

George (*to Clare*) You mean it was all *your* idea?

Clare Well I've known them for a long time, you see.

Jack *Who?*

Ruth My husband and I.

Jack (*disappointed*) You're not married, are you?

Ruth (*smiling*) Only in the game.

Clare (*to George*) Wives can feel neglected too, you know.

Jack *I'll* drink to that.

Nick Stone *me!*

Ruth (*to Jack*) Just a minute—we've forgotten about *you.*

Jack Me?

Ruth Now who could *you* be?

Jack (*referring to Jane*) I'm her *father.*

Nick Why not? Always wanted a *daughter*, didn't you?

Jane He's got *me* (*She takes Jack's arm*).

Ruth You're the father, then.

Jack Yes. And I let her down. All she wanted was someone she could look up to.

Nick *Right.* All *she* needed was a *father-figure?*

George (*aghast*) Father-figure?

Jane Well he could hardly call himself the great *lover.*

George (*dignified, hand to chest*) I have this rumble.

Clare So have *you.*

Jane (*to Ruth*) Rub some *Vick* on his feet.

Jack *I* used to rub Vick on Janey's chest.

Nick *Pervert!*

Jane The last thing I wanted to do was break up anyone's marriage.

Ruth Which is why you chose a married man.

Clare Wouldn't he *have* to be married if she . . .?

Ruth *Exactly.*

Jack I'd kill him if I ever met him.

George He might be rather nice.

Clare He *is.* (*Hastily*) I should think.

Ruth That's not the point.

George Isn't it?

Ruth She only went with him *because* he was married—because, deep-down, she knew he was unobtainable.

George (*at Jane*) You mean she didn't really *want* him?

Jane Not in the way *he* thought.

George (*getting angry*) Oh I *see*—so it's all a *game* is it?
Clare Of *course* it's a game. ("*Gaily*") We're having *fun!*
George *Fun?* Yes of course we are. (*He does his "laugh"*) So it seems as if
    this—girl—won't be seeing much more of this—father-figure, doesn't it?
Jane Apparently not.
Jack I'm pleased about that.
Nick That's right—take the easy way out.
Ruth I think this young man and his girl-friend should get married.
Nick } Rubbish! { *Speaking*
Jane }   { *together*
Nick Marriage is for women—men should have nothing to do with it.
George *Agreed.*
Clare I *beg* your pardon?
George (*his face dropping*) In the game—the game—only in the game.
Nick After all, what is a woman? Ninety-two percent *water.* (*To Jack*)
    You're in love with a drink on a stick.
Jane Why must you always be so *rude?*
Nick *Me* rude—ha!
Jane (*taking Jack's arm*) You'd better get to like him—you'll be seeing a
    lot more of him in the future.
Nick (*pointing at George*) He just said . . .
George (*quickly*) I just said—I thought I could smell lunch.
Clare Have we finished then?
George Game, set and match.
Ruth (*to Jane*) You've just saved yourself a stamp.
Clare Then let's have a pact—no more playing games—no more discussing
    other people's problems . . . (*To Nick*) Agreed?
Nick Agreed.
George (*to Jane*) Agreed?
Jane Agreed.
Nick (*to Jack*) Agreed?
Jack (*still the victim*) Agreed.
George Thank god for that. Come along everybody—lunch.

*Everyone stands—start collecting up their drinks, etc. George notices the
suitcase*

    Whose is that?

All movement stops

Nick Oh—that's mine.
George Ah. I thought it might have been *yours*, Jack.
Jack No—I didn't *bring* one.

They all start to move again

Nick *Jack?* I thought your name was *George?*
Jane } No . . . *this* is George . . . { *Speaking*
Clare }   { *together*

Jane and Clare move to George, each linking an arm through his. Suddenly they become aware of each other. They look from each other to George

George I know *another* very good game called Consequences . . .

George moves away from the women; Clare moves after him; Nick moves after Jane; Jack and Ruth move together; so that everyone is converging on George. George backs away, and falls backwards along the length of the sofa, as—

the CURTAIN falls

FURNITURE AND PROPERTY LIST

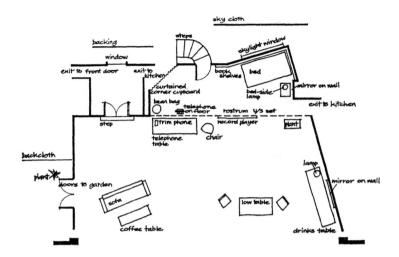

ACT I

SCENE 1

On stage: DRAWING-ROOM:
Sofa. *On it:* cushions
3 small chairs
Coffee table. *On it:* ashtray
Telephone table. *On it:* telephone, directories, ashtray, pencil, pad
Low occasional table. *On it:* ashtray
Drinks table. *On it:* lamp, whisky, gin, brandy, vodka, soda water, tonic water, various glasses, bottle opener, ice bucket, ashtray
Record player and records
Pot plant
On wall: mirror
Window curtains
Carpet

BEDSITTER:
Double bed and bedding. *Under it:* football scarf, rattle
Inflatable plastic chair. *On floor beside it:* telephone
Bookshelves (around bed). *In them:* stacks of books
Curtained corner cupboard. *In it:* Jane's clothes, hangers
Bedside cupboard. *In it:* mountain of junk, including set of chest expanders, artist's palette, oil brushes. *On top:* lamp, portable record player and records, Jane's handbag with money.
On wall above bed: reversible poster of bull-fight/notice: "Trespassers will be violated"
Scattered about room: books, crockery
On door: hook

Off stage: Plate with orange peel, quart bottle of beer **(Jane)**
             3 bunches of flowers, 2 large **(George)**
             Bottle of red wine **(George)**
             Flower pot **(Jane)**
             2 glasses and bottle opener **(Jane)**
             George's carpet slippers **(Clare)**
             Pile of books **(Nick)**
             Bottle of milk **(Nick)**
             Towel **(Nick)**

Personal: **Jane:** watch
             Ruth: cigarettes, lighter
             George: cigarettes, lighter
             Nick: key, cigarettes, matches

Scene 2

Strike: **DRAWING-ROOM:**
          Used glasses

          BEDSITTER:
          Bottle, used glasses

Set: **DRAWING-ROOM:**
          George's jacket on chair

          BEDSITTER:
          Alarm clock in suitcase under bed
          Jane's clothes in corner cupboard

Off stage: George's hat with flower in it
            Briefcase **(Ruth)**
            Package of sausages **(Nick)**

Scene 3

Strike: **BEDSITTER:**
          Sausages
          Alarm clock

Set: **DRAWING-ROOM:**
          Chest expanders behind sofa

          BEDSITTER:
          Glass of wine for **George**
          Open bottle of wine on cabinet

Off stage: Apron **(Jane)**
            Stick of celery **(George)**
            Bottle of milk and mug **(Nick)**
            Knitting **(Clare)**
            Tray of sandwiches **(Clare)**

ACT II

SCENE 1

Strike:
DRAWING-ROOM:
Tray of sandwiches
Knitting
Dirty glasses
Chest expanders

BEDSITTER:
Dirty glasses, milk bottle, mug

Set:
DRAWING-ROOM:
Replace small chair
Empty flower pot
Newspaper on sofa

BEDSITTER:
Bowl of water, basin, towel
Stolen ashtray on chair arm
Newspaper on bed cabinet

Off-stage:
Tray of sandwiches (**Clare**)
Small bunch of flowers (**Nick**)
½ bottle of Spanish red wine (**Nick**)
Kettle, full (**Jane**)

Personal:
Nick: address book

SCENE 2

Strike:
DRAWING-ROOM:
Tray of sandwiches
Dirty glasses

BEDSITTER:
Basin, bowl, towel

Set:
DRAWING-ROOM:
Hoover
Suitcase on table
Large tray by drinks cabinet
Check glasses in drinks cabinet
Dishes of nuts, pretzels, gherkins, etc. on drinks cabinet

BEDSITTER:
Suitcase with "frillies" on bed
Tatty suitcase under bed

Off stage:
Pair of bright pyjamas (**George**)
Torn vest used as duster (**Clare**)
Aerosol sprays (**George**)
Tin of grease, oily rag, air filter (**George**)
Box stacked with drinks and large packet of crisps (**George**)

Personal:
Jack: card

LIGHTING PLOT

Property fittings required: table lamps, wall brackets in drawing-room; pendant in bedsitter

Interior. A drawing-room and bedsitter. The same scene throughout

ACT I SCENE 1. Early evening

To open:	Artificial lighting on full in bedsitter Drawing-room in darkness	
Cue 1	Drawing-room telephone rings *Bring up spot on drawing-room telephone*	(Page 7)
Cue 2	Clare sighs *Fade drawing-room spot*	(Page 8)
Cue 3	Jane leans against door *Crossfade from bedsitter to full artificial lighting in drawing-room*	(Page 9)
Cue 4	George: "What!" *Crossfade from drawing-room to bedsitter*	(Page 17)
Cue 5	Nick exits *Lights up in drawing-room*	(Page 18)

ACT I SCENE 2. Morning

To open:	Bedsitter lighting on—daylight	
Cue 6	Nick exits *Crossfade from bedsitter to drawing-room—daylight*	(Page 22)
Cue 7	Bedsitter telephone rings *Bedsitter lighting up*	(Page 23)

ACT I SCENE 3. Evening

To open:	Bedsitter artificial lighting up	
Cue 8	George dials *Bring up drawing-room artificial lighting*	(Page 29)
Cue 9	Jane and George exit *Fade bedsitter lighting*	(Page 30)
Cue 10	Nick: " . . . she'll regret at any moment" *Bedsitter lighting up*	(Page 32)
Cue 11	George exits *Fade bedsitter lighting*	(Page 33)
Cue 12	Nick exits Bedsitter lighting up	(Page 33)
Cue 13	George exits *Fade bedsitter lighting*	(Page 35)
Cue 14	Clare: "*Knickers*" *Crossfade from drawing-room to bedsitter lighting*	(Page 38)
Cue 15	Jane exits *Crossfade from bedsitter to drawing-room lighting*	(Page 39)

Cue 16	**George** dials *Bedsitter lighting up*	(Page 41)

ACT II SCENE 1. Evening

To open:	Drawing-room artificial lighting on *Bedsitter in darkness*	
Cue 17	**Clare** turns off main lights *Snap off drawing-room lighting except for one lamp*	(Page 43)
Cue 18	**Clare** pushes Nick onto sofa *Crossfade from drawing-room to bedsitter artificial lighting*	(Page 45)
Cue 19	**Jane** enters *Crossfade from bedsitter to drawing-room lighting as at Cue 17*	(Page 48)
Cue 20	**Clare:** "Mickey *Mouse*?" *Crossfade from drawing-room to bedsitter lighting*	(Page 49)
Cue 21	**George** exits *Bring up drawing-room artificial lighting to full*	(Page 50)
Cue 22	**Nick** and **Clare** turn to telephone *Black-Out*	(Page 54)

ACT II SCENE 2. Morning

To open:	Black-Out	
Cue 23	**As scene opens** *Fade up bedsitter lighting only, to daylight*	(Page 54)
Cue 24	**Nick** exits *Crossfade to drawing-room lighting, daylight*	(Page 55)
Cue 25	**Clare** and **George** exit *Crossfade to bedsitter lighting*	(Page 56)
Cue 26	**Jane** exits *Bring up drawing-room lighting*	(Page 59)
Cue 27	**Jane** exits *Bring up drawing-room lighting*	(Page 61)

EFFECTS PLOT

ACT I

SCENE 1

Cue 1	**Jane** exits to kitchen *China crash*	(Page 3)
Cue 2	**Jane** replaces things in cupboard *Bedsitter doorbell rings*	(Page 3)
Cue 3	**Jane** reverses poster *Bedsitter doorbell rings*	(Page 3)
Cue 4	**George** dials *Drawing-room telephone rings*	(Page 7)
Cue 5	**Clare:** "... and run the bath" *Car arrives and stops*	(Page 13)
Cue 6	After **George** exits *Dog barks*	(Page 19)
Cue 7	**Nick:** "I *understand* ... I *understand* ..." *Bedsitter telephone rings*	(Page 20)

SCENE 2

Cue 8	**George** dials *Bedsitter telephone rings*	(Page 23)
Cue 9	**Clare** and **Ruth** exit *Bedsitter doorbell rings*	(Page 25)
Cue 10	**Nick:** "Place toad in hole..." *Bedsitter telephone rings*	(Page 26)

SCENE 3

Cue 11	**Nick** eats sandwich *Drawing-room telephone rings*	(Page 29)
Cue 12	**Jane** forces **George** on bed *Bedsitter telephone rings*	(Page 32)
Cue 13	**Nick** and **George** dial together *"Engaged" tone on both telephones*	(Page 35)
Cue 14	**Nick:** "... you mustn't worry." *House doorbell rings*	(Page 36)
Cue 15	**Ruth:** "Very dishy indeed." *Car arrives and stops*	(Page 37)
Cue 16	**Jane** is about to get into bed *Bedsitter telephone rings*	(Page 41)

ACT II

SCENE 1

Cue 17	As **Clare** switches off main lights *House doorbell rings*	(Page 43)

Cue 18	**Clare** puts on record *"Smoochy music" from radiogram*	(Page 44)
Cue 19	As lights fade *Music off*	(Page 45)
Cue 20	**Jane** puts on record *"Rolling Stones" number*	(Page 47)
Cue 21	As lights fade *Music off*	(Page 48)
Cue 22	**Clare** and **Jane** sit with newspapers *Sound of car starting, making short, noisy* *journey, stopping, door slamming*	(Page 51)

SCENE 2

Cue 23	Lights come up in bedsitter *Bedsitter doorbell rings*	(Page 56)
Cue 24	**George:** "Bloody *car* . . ." *Drawing-room telephone rings*	(Page 60)
Cue 25	**George** sings one of his rugby club songs *Bedsitter telephone rings*	(Page 60)
Cue 26	**Jane** rings off *House doorbell rings*	(Page 61)
Cue 27	**Clare:** ". . . written to Anna Raeburn." *House doorbell rings*	(Page 62)
Cue 28	**Clare:** "No, you don't!" *House doorbell rings*	(Page 64)
Cue 29	**Clare:** " . . . so *many* pills." *House doorbell rings*	(Page 64)
Cue 30	**Jane:** " . . . I think I might soon." *House doorbell rings*	(Page 66)
Cue 31	**Ruth** exits *House doorbell rings*	(Page 66)

MUSIC USE NOTE

Licensees are solely responsible for obtaining formal written permission from copyright owners to use copyrighted music in the performance of this play and are strongly cautioned to do so. If no such permission is obtained by the licensee, then the licensee must use only original music that the licensee owns and controls. Licensees are solely responsible and liable for all music clearances and shall indemnify the copyright owners of the play(s) and their licensing agent, Samuel French, against any costs, expenses, losses and liabilities arising from the use of music by licensees. Please contact the appropriate music licensing authority in your territory for the rights to any incidental music.

IMPORTANT BILLING AND CREDIT REQUIREMENTS

If you have obtained performance rights to this title, please refer to your licensing agreement for important billing and credit requirements.